Finding Family

Finding Family

RICK OUSTON

New Star Books
Vancouver
1994

To protect my mother, the names of my birth mother and father, and their relatives, have been changed.

Published by New Star Books Ltd., 2504 York Avenue, Vancouver, B.C., Canada V6K 1E3. All rights reserved. No part of this work may be reproduced or used in any form or by any means — graphic, electronic, or mechanical — without the prior written permission of the publisher. Any request for photocopying or other reprographic copying must be sent in writing to the Canadian Reprography Collective (Cancopy), 312 - 214 King Street West, Toronto, Ontario M5H 2S6.

Publication of this book is made possible by grants from the Canada Council, the Canadian Heritage Book Publishing Industry Development Program, and the Cultural Services Branch, Province of British Columbia

Printed and bound in Canada by Best Gagné Book Manufacturers
1 2 3 4 5 98 97 96 95 94
First printing, July 1994

Canadian Cataloguing in Publication Data

Ouston, Rick, 1955-

  Finding family

  ISBN 0-921586-31-0

  1. Ouston, Rick, 1955- 2. Birthparents — Canada — Identification. 3. Adoptees — Canada — Biography. I. Title.
HV874.82.O97A3 1994   362.82'98'092   C94-910279-2

For all the secret mothers

Finding Family

One

M y sister Sharon was back home. She'd gone away, part way through the last year of high school, to live with a distant relative in a town called Hope. A few weeks later she came back home to Vancouver, and the curtains were drawn.

They remained closed for months, cloaking the living room in a constant grey. My sister and I played a lot of cribbage those months, having been indoctrinated into the game by a maiden aunt as soon as we were able to count. We'd sprawl across Sharon's bed, dealing the cards again and again, moving plastic pegs around the board, determining a winner, beginning anew. Had we counted the games we played, it would have determined how many games of crib it took to have a baby. I was eleven. She was pregnant. The word was never said.

Teenagers didn't get pregnant in 1967. Particularly Catholic teenagers. Marriage was sanctified by the church, and you couldn't have a child out of wedlock. The church taught us so. I thought it was a physical impossibility: if the church says you can't, then you can't. About as straightforward as going to hell if you sin, or the inherent goodness of priests.

Sharon told her little brother he was not to tell anyone she was at home. It was a secret, and secrets are for keeping. She was ashamed. It showed. She cried a lot. I loved her and I didn't want her to hurt. There's not much you can do when you're eleven except help your older sister kill time playing cards.

Ronald Norman Ouston was born May 27, 1967. A few days later Sharon came home from the hospital, alone. The curtains were opened, light shone in the living room and it was as if Ronald Norman Ouston never existed.

As if.

Legally, the infant known as Ronald Norman Ouston did not exist. Shortly after the birth, Sharon signed papers giving the child up for adoption. With those papers, any rights, societal, moral or legal, that Sharon had to the son she bore were extinguished. What happened to baby Ronnie is anyone's guess. Likely he was adopted by a good Catholic family, a couple unable to conceive their own children, and he was raised and loved as if he were their own child.

As if.

A decade earlier, the same process had been applied to me. I was adopted. Sharon was too. So was sister Lorraine. All three Ouston kids were adopted, and now the Ouston kids continued the family tradition of having babies that would not be raised by their parents. Like the cribbage game, endlessly around the board, the cycle of birth and secret childbirth continued. Where do babies come from, mommy? We chose you, honey, our mommy Ann would say. It was an easier out than messy talk of eggs and sperm and nasty body bits.

There were two kinds of babies, adopted ones and real ones. We knew that, Sharon, Lorraine and I. Adopted ones weren't really the same as real ones. They couldn't compare eye color or heights to ancestors, or talk about being just like uncle this or auntie that. Grandmothers treated adopted kids differently, we knew this too. Our nana, Ann's mother, had more candies for our cousins than she had for us. She'd give them extra when she knew we weren't looking, but we were looking anyway and I think she knew. It wasn't a big deal, really. An extra treat here and there, more invitations for sleepovers to real grandchildren than adopted ones, that's the way things are. Now Sharon had a baby and now she didn't, and that baby would grow up with someone else and those someone elses would be his family and his new grandmother might or might not treat him differently from her real grandchildren.

The summer after Ronald was born, Fred and Ann Ouston took me to a movie called *Doctor Speaks Out*. It was recommended by the Catholic church as a good way to teach your kids about sex. In the lobby of the theatre, registered nurses treated film patrons troubled by the scenes, in living color, of babies being born. Tiny human babies, delivered naturally and by caesarean section, seen on screen for the first time. No storks, no cabbage patches, just lots of goo and yelling. The film answered, for the first time for me, the question of where babies came from. From inside there. At home, I asked Fred Ouston, my adoptive father, how they got there in the first place.

"You know the pumpkins we grow in the compost box for Halloween?" he said. "Well, on the pumpkin, there's a male flower, and a female flower." He held the fingers of one hand in the shape of a cup. He scrunched the fingers of his other hand together and placed them inside the open hand. "The male flower fits inside the female flower," he said.

I did not have a clue what he was talking about. But that ended the discussion, Fred satisfied that he had told me what he knew and what I needed to know. It was likely the same story young Fred heard from his own father years earlier. I'll never know. Fred died the next year. He was a carpenter, working on a grain elevator on the Vancouver waterfront. He fell from a scaffolding, landed on his head, died on the spot. The family he built died with him. The clean smell of wheat haunts me still.

As a couple, Ann and Fred Ouston meshed admirably. He stood six-foot-four, she scraped five-ten. An attack of the mumps at puberty robbed Fred of his ability to make babies. All the plumbing worked, as they say, it just came to naught. He was the emotional one, full of dreams, thwarted by a bad back and a crummy job that never quite pulled in enough to go around. Tears, at night, from Fred, when the kids were supposedly sleeping and not hearing. Money troubles. Ann was the homemaker, the realist, working nights as a cleaning lady and summers at the salmon cannery on the Fraser River, making do, running a home. Popular at church functions, Fred made the friends, Ann did her best to make sure everyone got fed. His yin to her yang, he called her honey and at weddings we watched as they danced, Fred impossibly limber for a big man, Ann proud of her husband, loving the dance.

The earliest memories my sisters and I had were of being called "my adopted baby" by Fred and Ann. The wisdom of the day, in the 1940s and 50s, was that adoptive parents should tell their children the truth of their adoption, instead of keeping it a secret that a drunken uncle might blurt out during a family function. We knew we were adopted, and that adoption made us different. Depending on your point of view, "different" can be pejorative, as in alien; or good, as in special. Fred and

Ann also avoided the temptation to badmouth our original parents, or "birth parents" as they were called. While some adoptive parents spoke darkly of "bad mothers who didn't want you" or parents who abandoned their babies like so much trash, we were told only that our parents "couldn't" raise us, and that they made sure their babies would get a good upbringing by giving them up for adoption. In truth, Ann and Fred knew nothing more about the backgrounds of their babies than the church workers had told them, and the church workers told them little. Baby Ricky was born Paul Anthony Griffin, they knew that much, and his heritage was said to be Irish, English and Scottish. End of story.

We were adopted kids, but Dad was our dad and Mom was our mom, and we didn't have their height or their eyes or their anything but their love. And that was enough. When Fred died, Ann died on the inside, mourning the man she'd loved. She was left with kids they'd adopted, a widow's pension, and the life-insured mortgage. For the first time there was enough money to make ends meet, barely, with no treats; but the ends of her life dangled, heart strings no longer anchored.

Her children, now fatherless, ran wild at times, respecting their grieving mother, employing lies and evasions so as not to upset her with the truth. Lorraine ran with a motorcycle club, Sharon got caught passing bad cheques, both married the men who fathered their babies, born a few months after their parents walked down the aisle, the tiny fetuses listening to the Wedding March. I tinkered with drugs and petty crime, giving up the underworld after getting arrested and nearly shot for possession of a replica handgun that the Vancouver Police Department thought was going to be used to shoot a real cop. Handcuffs biting into wrists in the back seat of a police cruiser are a pretty good test of a young man's mettle. It taught this young man he had the right stuff to be a wimp. I am forever thankful to the cops for not shooting me, to birth control for not making me a father, to the journalism school I attended for accepting me without a high-school diploma and for teaching me how to think — to think of questions, and search for answers.

The questions I had were these: Who was my mother? Who was my father? Why was I, and how did I come to be?

Ann was my mother in all but in blood, and Fred was my father. They both raised me as well and as long as they could. But once past my teens, I remembered the cribbage games and the tears of my sister Sharon, and wondered if the woman who gave me birth cried because of the life she carried within. Had she hidden in a darkened home, played crib with her baby brother? Did she think of the baby she'd had, the way Sharon still thought of hers, and cry some more?

Simple questions. The answers would be years in coming.

*I*t is estimated by those who count such things that 2 to 3 per cent of the North American population is adopted. The numbers aren't firm because for years no one really counted them. *Us.* You don't count something which officially didn't happen. Babies have been adopted for as long as babies have been born, but it is a process cloaked in secrecy and shame. Good girls didn't do it, and if they did, they didn't talk about it.

The ancient Sumerians exacted a particularly harsh penalty for anyone who spoke of another's adoption: they cut off the offender's tongue. Crude, but effective. Tongue-carving has passed out of favor since then, but adoption is still something that good families don't much discuss. The reasoning is quite simple: most of the babies who were adopted were born out of wedlock. "Illegitimate" children. Bastards. Obviously born of substandard stock, their mothers harlots or worse.

There are always exceptions, of course. Babies born to large families of meagre means who just couldn't afford another mouth to feed were parceled off to orphanages for adoption by parents who could afford them. Native Indian kids were scooped off reserves by well-intentioned but poorly informed white social workers who didn't recognize that the culture of First Nations people afforded an extended family who would watch out for their needs. Instead, the social workers would deem a home to be unsatisfactory and hustle the children into orphanages for eventual transplanting across the country and around the world. Add to those the children adopted by step-parents and grandparents, and children created from the crimes of rape and incest, or from commercial prostitution, and the numbers grow.

But for the most part, babies who were adopted came from mothers who were not married, usually mothers in their teens who committed the sin of falling in love and having sex. The church helped out, various denominations opening their own homes for unwed mothers to ensure that the babies would be raised in faiths consistent with their own. Family doctors matched up childless patients with the offspring of teenaged patients, and social welfare agencies helped those with nowhere else to go. In the days before birth control pills and legalized abortion, when single motherhood just wasn't an option, adoption was often the only recourse for pregnant young women. Society said these women — sometimes just girls — had sinned, so what they had done wasn't talked about, and often was not even recorded. Hence the statisticians just don't have much to go on. And many adopting parents, themselves unable to conceive children, kept their adoptions bathed in secrecy, hiding the perceived shame of their "incompleteness." The result is secrecy on both sides of the adoption equation, leaving number crunchers with little to crunch.

In Canada, the National Adoption Study performed by researchers at the University of Guelph in 1993 confined itself to the period between 1980 and 1990. Dr. Michael Sobol, who oversaw the report, told me that the figures for any time earlier are not available, either because they rest in secret records held by church or state, or because they just weren't maintained. Sobol's study referred to earlier estimates that adoptees make up 2 to 3 per cent of the population, but no one knows for sure what the numbers are. The study did find that, of the women who placed children for adoption between 1980 and 1990, almost 75 per cent were between the ages of fifteen and nineteen. "Almost half (46 per cent) indicated she was Protestant, 29 per cent said Catholic and 15 per cent said no religious affiliation," the report said.

Interestingly, a large number of service providers surveyed by the report said that "a typical characteristic of birth mothers was that they were adopted themselves. One possible explanation for the relatively high proportion of birth mothers who were adopted is that, through the process of placing a child, they are seeking to understand and normalize the fact that they themselves were placed for adoption."

Whether that played any role in Sharon's relinquishment of her baby could take years on a therapist's couch to figure out. She does recall, however, that keeping the curtains closed was her idea, not Fred and Ann's. "I was ashamed of myself, and I didn't want them to feel shamed. I didn't want anyone to know, because I didn't want them to be hurt."

She had talked about her pregnancy with our parents, and they explored the options: raising the child herself, Fred and Ann raising him as their own. It would still be a year before abortion was legalized in Canada, and Ann remembered girlhood friends butchered and dying at the hands of back-street abortionists in her youth. The Catholic church taught that abortion was tantamount to murder, so the seventeen-year-old Sharon didn't really consider abortion an option.

Today's prospective adoptive parents, facing waiting lists of seven years and longer for a child they can call their own, blame easier access to abortion for the shortage of available babies. But, in fact, the National Adoption Study found fewer young women are choosing abortion as a way to resolve an unwanted pregnancy than ever before, despite the growth of private abortion clinics across the country. Instead, more young girls are keeping their babies, knowing they can count on societal support instead of being shunned. That's bad news for people who can't conceive their own children, but a lot less stress on women in the 1990s who don't have to suffer the guilt and loss of relinquishing a baby.

Even abortion causes much less trauma to women than giving up a child, according to a study by Paul Sachdev, a professor of social work at the University of Newfoundland in St. John's. In his book *Sex, Abortion and Unmarried Women* he writes, "Soon after the abortion, most women (78.6 per cent) felt relief and satisfaction. Long-term psychological reactions of guilt or depression were rare."

It seems incongruous writing these words, an adoptee pondering the benefits of abortion over adoption. Had the law been different in 1955, the year of my birth, the fetus who became this writer might never have been born. But if abortion had been an option for the unknown woman who was my mother, her life may have been different, perhaps much better, and any argument from me would be moot because I would not have existed. The abortion debate will likely rage on forever, and will not be resolved in these pages. The fact is that I, and tens of thousands of people like me, were born prior to the change in abortion availability — unwanted, unplanned for, given up at birth. Now, as adults, we struggle with our differentness. For too long we have struggled in silence.

Perhaps our problem seems tiny to other established special-interest groups. Adult children of alcoholics, incest survivors, the disabled, rape victims, all have a valid and powerful claim on suffering. Many people who were adopted as infants were raised by spectacular parents who loved us, cared for us, gave us homes and support and a name. What do we have to complain about?

But others who have studied the adoption phenomenon attribute to us a "primal wound," in the words of author Nancy N. Verrier. We did not bond with a mother. That lack of bonding, of completion, can stick with adoptees throughout their lives, according to psychologists. It can manifest itself in adulthood as an unwillingness or inability to share, to commit, to trust. The trauma caused by separation of baby and mother may be little but a tickle in the back of the brain, perhaps not even felt at all. Or felt as an absence — something that is *not* there.

As an adult, intellectually I knew that there was no cause to complain about being abandoned, the word so beloved of psychiatrists. There must have been a reason why I was given up for adoption, and that's all in the past, what's done is done.

But at times, growing up, and as a grown-up, in the night when it was dark, I felt more alone than it is fair to feel.

And society said, Don't talk about it. You had parents who raised you. Don't hurt them. Don't talk about it. Don't even think about it. It is your secret.

To perpetuate the secrecy, provinces and states passed their own adoption laws, codifying for the courts how babies born to others would be "as if" born to the adoptive parents. Backgrounds would be dismissed, the fact of the adoption sealed by the courts, and the best interests of the child — and of the adopting parent — would be protected.

Also dismissed were the interests of the birth mother. But, since she had been a bad girl, no one attached much importance to extending rights to someone with a big scarlet letter on her forehead.

All this played successfully for a long time. Father Knew Best, Ozzie and Harriet didn't have any adopted kids, Patty Duke never got knocked up and Archie juggled the affections of Betty and Veronica without apparently ever reaching second base. Premarital sex — remember the term? — wasn't discussed ... but it went on in back seats and back yards and back bedrooms, spawning generations of unwanted babies who grew up and wondered where they came from, but who were told not to talk about it for fear of being branded a bastard. That was until the civil rights clamor of the sixties, when the disenfranchised found a voice and demanded rights. Women spoke out, so did ethnic minorities and the disabled. The bastards took a little bit longer.

By the mid-1970s, pockets of organized resistance grew

up around the "as if" theory. In Canada, change was spear-headed by a feisty housewife named Joan Vanstone, an adoptee herself who spent years tracking down her own mother. When Vanstone finally found her, she learned her mother had died just months earlier. Vanstone was deeply saddened, and not a little angry. The secrecy around her adoption meant that Joan Vanstone would never be able to speak to her mother, to hold her, to learn of her genetic heritage, to tell her mother she loved her. Vanstone's life, like that of most adoptees, had been relatively normal insofar as her adoptive parents were like any other parents, some good, some bad, most somewhere in the middle.

Vanstone took on a mission: to help other adoptees avoid the loss she felt by assisting them in their searches for their roots before it was too late. She imported a U.S. creation called Parent Finders, a relatively simple scheme by which adoptees and relinquishing parents could register their names and birthdates and places, hoping the other side might also register. If there was a match — child and parent on the register — a reunion would take place.

These were guerrilla tactics, a way to circumvent the power of the state. Vanstone's mission spread through word of mouth, along sort of an adoption underground, with meetings in living rooms and community halls. Sharon heard about one such meeting in 1976, and took me along. She knew neither her heritage nor what happened to her son. Hers was a double search for resolution. By now I was married, attending college, thinking about the world and my place in it. The fact of my adoption hadn't preyed on my mind, but had always been there, niggling, a little thing that set me apart from most. From time to time Sharon and I talked about the unknowns of our lives.

We knew our original names and birthdays, information

contained in the adoption orders that had made us officially Oustons. Ann and Fred kept the adoption orders in their grey steel box for special papers, and allowed us access to them from our earliest memories. One day you might want to find your birth parents, they had said. Sharon was born Laura Roberta McCready on July 20, 1949. My original name was Paul Anthony Griffin, born September 10, 1955. That was all we knew.

Now, Vanstone offered help. And hints to get around the wall of secrecy.

Most provincial governments had already buckled under pressure from activists like Vanstone and had started releasing some information about the backgrounds of adoptees to those who asked. They called it "non-identifying information," sanitized, sans facts and names, little more than a sop, but something. But you had to know who to ask, and how. Vanstone spent thousands of hours volunteering her time to assist adoptees in obtaining that scanty assistance, and had developed a trove of investigative techniques of her own. With her help, I applied for an interview with a social worker, and started searching through the past.

*T*he thing that angers most adoptees seeking the story of their lives is that usually there is a file, fat with information, sitting somewhere, which could answer all the questions we have. Trouble is, we don't have access to that file. Under the legislation governing adoption in all Canadian provinces and most U.S. states, that file is sealed. Its secret contents are guarded zealously lest they fall into the wrong hands — like the hands of the individual whose life is contained in that file. The information came usually from interviews with the pregnant mother, usually little more than a child herself, who responded to questions about her history to assist the social worker in "placing" the soon-to-be infant in the best possible home, matching religious and ethnic affiliations with prospective adoptive parents. Usually the file folder contains the names of the adoptee's mother and father, and often of grandparents, aunts and uncles. Home towns, family histories, addresses, phone numbers, all were recorded by social workers, governmental or church, jotted down on note pads, typewritten later, carefully tucked away. Then locked away. To do otherwise, to allow adoptees access to the facts of their lives, would contravene the law that says once adopted, the individual is "as if born to" the adopting parents.

Looking for the facts of your life? Tough. The law says it's none of your business. Legally, there's little that can be done about it, unless lawmakers change the law. Usually, bad laws do get changed, eventually. Imagine if the members sitting in your provincial or state capital passed a law saying that dogs were "as if" cats. Life would go on pretty much as usual, despite the best intentions of the legislators. Dogs would not use kitty litter. They would refuse to act coy and disinterested in human companions and would continue their slavish acts of devotion and affection. They would come when called, and not just when they felt like it. In short, dogs would not be cats, no matter what the law said. And adoptees are not born of adoptive parents, no matter what the law says. They don't have the same genetic make-up, coloring, size, medical or genealogical histories. Nevertheless, the bureaucrats and drones who control access to information are governed by the laws passed and perpetuated by their political masters. So, when the masters say something shall remain a secret, it does. While Sumerians lopped off tongues, modern North American bureaucrats carry out a more sensitive policy of simply ordering tongues sealed, and everybody goes about their business. The files remain wherever they're stored, tantalizing but out of reach.

The files remained in church archives and orphanage basements until provincial and state governments took over adoptions in the 1960s and 70s. (The exception is in the province of Québec, where records continue to be retained by regional social and church services offices.) Social workers can look at the files; the people whom the files are about cannot. It's as simple and simplistic as that.

When an adoptee seeks his or her non-identifying information, a social worker pulls the file out of storage, reads it cover to cover, learns everything the file contains, then writes a sterilized account that will be given to the adoptee. No names, no towns. But when you've got nothing, a little something seems like a big improvement.

Ann and Fred Ouston had always told me what they had been told: father Irish, mother Scottish and English, nothing more. I felt certain that the bureaucracy would be able to provide at least a bit more than that. In those pre-recessionary times, when governmental offices were properly staffed, it took only a few days to receive the social worker's report, to visit the office and pick up the dribs and drabs culled from the file. Currently, some provinces have backlogs of three years and more to provide this service. Adoptees are, by tacit decision of their legislatures, essentially told to shut up, sit back, take a number and wait ... and some day, some year, someone might get to your request. We, the politicians in effect say, have better things to do.

This is what the non-identifying information told me:

You were born September 10, 1955, in Vancouver, at 7:42 p.m. You weighed seven pounds four ounces.

Your birth mother was not a very communicative person and unfortunately not much help was offered her by the worker. She tended to keep to herself and then evade issues when things became too much for her.

Your mother was born Jan. 21, 1934. She was described as a very attractive looking girl, petite, five feet two inches in height and one hundred and nine pounds. She had dark hair, brown eyes and small features. She was of English-Irish racial origin. She completed Grade ten at seventeen and worked as a sales clerk and telephone operator.

The letter goes on to say that my mother had many brothers and sisters, "about whom very little information was obtained." Her father died at the age of 62 in 1952.

After your birth, your mother revealed that she and your father had an older child who had been placed for adoption in Nova Scotia in 1954. This child was a normal, well developed little girl whose adoption had been completed in 1955.

Your birth parents knew each other when your father was stationed in Newfoundland, Canada as a member of the American Air Force and your mother worked on the base as a telephone operator. They had a long relationship which your mother hoped would culminate in marriage. However, when your father failed to come to Vancouver after your birth to discuss this, your mother requested that you be placed for adoption.

One can only guess that she suddenly left Vancouver to return to Newfoundland because she may have heard your father had likewise returned there. She did not but the Agency knew her address for several months and claimed that she had been "moving around."

Your birth father, as you know, was of Jewish and Scottish origin.

He was born March 29, 1932, in the States. After two years university, he enlisted in the Air Force where he was a Radar Mechanic. Your mother said that he was musical and that he appeared to be of "superior intelligence." She described him as being five feet eleven inches in height, one hundred and eighty pounds, with dark brown hair, brown eyes, medium complexion and with "round features." She said he was pleasant and jovial and that his health was good. His parents were separated. His father, aged fifty-six, had a "business" in California and his mother, age fifty-five, owned a fur store in New York City. He had one married sister, age twenty-nine.

And that was that.

The story of a life, mine, or at least how mine came to be.

Again and again I reread this "non-identifying information" about my mother. She was "not a very communicative person". In whose eyes? What does this mean? Did the worker of the day, back in 1955, write this, or was it an observation of the 1976 functionary? And if an observation, based on what?

I try to form a mental picture of a "very attractive" girl, but with nothing more to go on, no picture comes. What are "small features"? When most people think of the word "mother," a picture comes to mind. When I think of mother, I think of Ann Ouston. When I think of this woman who gave me birth and who was my mother, I cannot see a face.

Oh, by the way, the letter continues, they had another child. A girl. You have a sister. I have a sister. I wonder who she is? Or where she is? She was adopted the year I was born. I wonder if she knows she's adopted. I wonder if she cares she has a brother.

Daddy was a Yankee. A serviceman. My father had done "it" with my mother, and she got pregnant, and he did not do the honorable thing and marry her. Not even after she got pregnant again. In my neighborhood, you were supposed to marry the girl when she got pregnant. Luckily birth control pills and access to abortion made those marriages less common today. Daddy was an American. Daddy was a jerk. Sigh. But it was a long time ago, and he was in the Army. Maybe he was just being a guy, a horny guy doing horny-guy things that I, after all, had done too. I can see a picture in my mind, a generic man-shape, shrugging over a beer and a meeting with his son, saying, Well, y'know, things happen. I might meet this man one day. It would be just like two guys getting together over a drink, talking manly stuff. There would be no recriminations. I'd just like to know what kind of man he is, about his background and his life. Then, after learning about him, I might punch his lights out. Or maybe just shake hands and walk away, head held high, walking like a man.

"One can only guess" what happened to my mother, the letter says. I have to reread this paragraph several times. I do, and still don t know what it means. One can only guess? Why? Why a guess? What is the guess based on? What information is in the file, or not in the file, that has led a faceless bureaucrat, trying to be helpful, to make a guess? How accurate is this guess? Why is a bureaucrat guessing about my life? The letter isn't saying that my mother vanished, but it seems to be saying she did. I guess the writer of the non-identifying information is trying to be gentle. Or something. The letter writer is guessing about me, about my mother, about my father. This isn't helpful.

Oh yeah, and by the way your father was half Jewish. I had read about Jews. They were in the Bible, and in the news once in a while about Israel and stuff, but I had never met one. A Jew? My father was a Jew? But Ann and Fred were told he was Scottish, and just Scottish. It appears that the Catholic family services social worker of the day had decided to sanitize the heritage of the baby the Oustons were adopting. I guess the Catholics felt that having Jewish blood was a black mark against this orphan, something best left unsaid. I don't even know what a Jew is, and now I am one, or at least partially. Funny, I don't feel any different.

And he was musical. Hey, me too! Like father, like son, eh? Maybe he plays the harmonica and sings bad Elvis imitations just like me. And "superior intelligence." Yeah, that makes sense. I was always top of the class in school, until I got bored and stopped doing schoolwork. But ... the information apparently comes from mom, whoever she is, and I doubt that she would have described the father of her child as an idiot even if it happened to be true. Yessiree, Mrs. Church Social Worker, I got knocked up by a real moron. No, she would probably have thought he was pretty bright, whether he was or not. This is not much help.

She said he was pleasant and jovial. Oh, she must have liked him then. This comes as a surprise, seeing as how she had two of his children. And he's one of 250 million Americans. End of the story of my life, official version, culled and devoid of fact. Access to more, denied. I have a sister. I wonder who she is. I have a little mother, five-foot-two, and she had brothers and sisters, but I already figured that. There was a father, an American, half-Jewish. No names, no places. Surely the file contains much more. But the file is sealed, and with it, the past.

A nn Ouston, née Thompson, had just one sibling, James. It was he, the man we called Uncle Jimmy, who was my godfather, entrusted to ensure that young Ricky would be raised in the Catholic church if, God forbid, Ann and Fred died while I was still an infant. It's tradition in the Roman Catholic church to have godfathers and godmothers who "sponsor" a child at baptism, that indoctrination into the faith which includes a ritual cleansing of original sin. My baptismal certificate said Jimmy's wife Catherine was my godmother, the co-sponsor. We called her Auntie Kay.

The baptismal certificate was a fraud, albeit a well-intentioned one. While Jimmy and Kay had agreed to take on the onerous job of raising a child in the event of untimely deaths, they were not present at my baptism, despite the claim on the baptismal certificate.

This is what the document from the Church of St. John the Apostle says:

> *This is to certify that Richard James Ouston child of Annie and Fred Ouston born in Vancouver on the 10th day of September, 1955 was Baptized on the 13th day of October 1955 according to the Rite of the Roman Catholic Church by the Rev. M.R. Hanley the Sponsors being James Thompson, Catherine Thompson as appears from the Baptismal Register of the Church, Dated August 12, 1957 [signed] Mr. R. Hanley Pastor.*

It was Parent Finders' Joan Vanstone who pointed out the discrepancy in the document: the baptism took place October 13, 1955, but the certificate was dated almost two years later. Although the certificate claimed to contain the information "as appears from the Baptismal Register," in October 1955 my name was not Richard James Ouston. Indeed, as near as we could learn from the original adoption order, my name had been Paul Anthony Griffin when I was baptised.

The baptismal certificate had been updated, altered from the original record to register the fact of my adoption. Although the Ten Commandments rule out lying in general, it appeared that the church, like everyone else in society, felt that a little white fib while updating documentation could avoid the stigma of an illegitimate birth.

If the church had updated its records, Vanstone reasoned, it likely still retained the original information in its registry. And it was possible that the original notation might include the name of a "birth" parent, or maybe both parents, or clues which could lead to tracking them down. Good Catholic girls got their babies baptized into the church, even if those babies were born out of wedlock. Perhaps my mother was there, back in 1955, holding her son while the priest poured holy water over my forehead. Perhaps her name appeared in the spot where it said "child of." Or maybe the original baptismal sponsors might be recorded. Perhaps the church could be tricked into releasing the information held so long, so diligently. While the provincial government kept its records sealed by legislative dictate, church records were still maintained by kindly old pastors in neighborhood churches. St. John the Apostle Church was a short drive across the city. I made the drive, arriving unannounced, finding the current priest inside the church taking care of priestly duties, and told him I needed my baptismal certificate to replace a lost one.

"And my name, Father, is Paul Anthony Griffin," I told him.

A lie, to a man of the cloth. Indeed, a sin similar to that perpetrated by the religious document handlers years earlier. The ethicists will argue that one sinful transgression does not cancel out another. Two wrongs don't make a right. But if the only way to right the wrong inherent under the "as if born to" rule was to lie, then damn the Hail Marys, full speed ahead.

And anyway, I'd lost my faith in the church years earlier. If I was to fry in hell for using a previous name, so be it.

"The registry is confidential," the priest said. "I'll have to look it up."

Damn, thought I, blaspheming in my heart in the House of God. I'd hoped to be able to look over the priest's shoulder, perhaps catching a glimpse of the original records, with the original names. Now that was not going to happen. My only hope was that the priest might confuse the original version of the records with the updated information and let something slip past.

The priest walked away, into a back room, and emerged a few minutes later, carrying a piece of paper.

"Thank you," I said. Out of the church, around the corner, lighting a cigarette and opening the document copied from the original register.

"Paul Anthony Ouston," it called me. The priest had gotten confused. He'd failed to record the fact that my name had been changed.

However, on the line where it said "child of," the priest had written Fred and Annie Ouston. He'd seen through my subterfuge.

Almost.

In the space left for "sponsors," Uncle Jimmy and Auntie Kay were forgotten. In their place, the priest had written the name of a "Mrs. B. Williscroft." There was nothing to indicate who she might be, or might have been.

A friend of my birth mother? A social worker, maybe

a church worker? Perhaps a nurse from the hospital where I was born. It had been St. Paul's in Vancouver, another good religious institution. Whoever she was, she had probably held the tiny baby who was me, all those years ago. She may have stood beside my mother, whoever she was, maybe holding her hand. She may know the name of the woman who was my mother; perhaps she knows everything.

But now, twenty years later, Mrs. B. Williscroft proved elusive. Local telephone books found no Bs listed under the surname. There were other Williscrofts, but none said they knew of a Mrs. B who was around in 1955. The provincial ministry of social services wouldn't tell me if a Mrs. B. Williscroft had once worked in the adoption business — "those records are confidential, sir," — and the Roman Catholic archives reported that all its records relating to adoptions had been seized by the provincial government a few years earlier. If Mrs. B had worked for the church, her records were also tightly guarded.

It was a blind alley, this baptismal record. This time. As it turned out, a similar document would later prove key to unlocking a huge part of the puzzle that was my beginnings. A dozen years would pass before I figured it out.

Two

This is when adoptees feel a need to actively chase down their roots: when they're ready. That's the observation of Parent Finders' Joan Vanstone, who has worked with thousands of adoptees and relinquishing parents. For some it's a burning need from an early age, a consuming passion that colors their entire being, a sense that they'll never feel whole — perhaps never feel at all — until they know the facts of their births. For others, their adoption is a minor note, ringing softly in the background music of their lives, barely audible, until maturity or crisis carries the adoption into crescendo.

Still others feel no need for search and reunion. Some studies indicate that male adoptees are four times less likely to search than their female counterparts. It's likely a "man" thing, a feeling of "I'm a big boy now and I don't need a mommy, especially two mommies." Women outnumber men by a similar ratio at adoptee support groups, historically because they are taught to be more in contact with their feelings, and to talk about what they're feeling, instead of bottling their emotions.

Whatever the case, adoptive parents should feel reassurance from the findings of the 1993 Adoption in Canada study, which concluded that "Search and reunion [are] no longer seen as being reflective of adoption failure but as a viable means of resolving past losses and as steps towards the development of a mature adult identity." In jurisdictions such as Israel, Britain and New Zealand, where adoption records are open to adoptees searching for their pasts, surveys of the searchers found no animosity toward adoptive parents — just a need to know the unknown.

My first stumbling steps toward unearthing the past stopped almost as soon as they had begun. Marriage and journalism occupied my time and my thoughts. There was always the knowledge of being different, of being envious of those who had connections to a family tree, thoughts that only bubbled to the surface of consciousness from time to time, but they were always there. The thoughts were accompanied by a vague sense of being alone, off to the side, unable to feel a part of the community — feeling, instead, apart and abandoned.

For a dozen years, however, my little file on adoption sat barely touched. Whoever my parents were, they had not registered with Parent Finders, so it was obvious they weren't eager to make contact with their ill-begotten son. Nor had the unknown sister registered, which meant she might not care about her adoption, or might not even know about it.

It took a classic midlife crisis to kick me into an active search. First my marriage ended, then the career collapsed.

In the summer of 1988, my bosses at the Canadian Broadcasting Corporation gave me extra vacation time as a bonus for doing what they felt was a good job as assignment editor of the regional supper-hour news show. After several years as the station's investigative reporter and TV commercial poster boy — "The NewsCentre's Rick Ouston, for the best news you'll see all day," intoned the TV ad — the promotion to the job of assigning reporters, cameramen and producers felt natural. Ratings climbed, and executive producer Helen Slinger worked out the extended vacation arrangement for her overworked assignment editor in one of her last acts at the station before moving on to work independently. She also finagled a short sabbatical for me at the University of Western Ontario for some advance training in media law. A contract for the next season would be ready to sign upon my return.

Snorkeling in Maui, baseball games in Toronto, fine dining in Montréal, a stop-over at the farm in Manitoba, intensive legal studies and Animal House-partying with twenty other newsies from across the country. I returned invigorated, ready for another season. Not ready to learn that since Slinger's departure and during my vacation there were new bosses with a new news mandate — stories would be produced in a minute-thirty, "and a minute-six if you can." After being wooed to the station to do long-form in-depth research, the one-time poster boy and award-winning reporter would now chase fire engines. I quit.

And found myself, for the first time in a dozen years, without a job, without a public profile. Freelancing and teaching would pay the meagre bills, but it felt as if the profession of journalism, something I had valued as a calling, like the priesthood, had turned against me. There were awards on the wall, a scrapbook plastered with clippings, usually a free beer proffered by a colleague at the Vancouver Press Club ... and not much else. I'd invested everything in journalism, putting news stories ahead of personal life, ahead of family, ahead even of my now-shattered marriage. The dividend hardly seemed worthwhile.

My departure from CBC made a few headlines in the local press. Long-time friend and confidante Wendy Ratcliffe read the stories and gave me a call. We'd occupied adjacent stools at the Press Club long into too many nights, sharing stories about secret fears and dreams and failed love affairs and futures. Wendy is brash, loud and opinionated, a condition exacerbated obnoxiously, wonderfully when she's satisfying her insatiable appetite for beer. Alone, talking privately, she is also capable of great insight and caring. We met at a nearby neighborhood pub, Wendy adopting the role that good friends play, that of counselor, crying towel, and beer-buyer as her friend looked blankly into the bottom of a pint mug. It felt like everything I'd touched had turned to mush. The career goals we'd discussed during the years had been met. The question now was: now what?

There was the land in Manitoba I'd bought years earlier, thinking maybe one day to farm there to subsidize a writing career. But farming is hard work for little pay, and I'd learned to hate manual labor. Maybe just move to another city and give news another try. But that meant a move from Vancouver, a place that feels like home. Nowhere else would feel the same. I care about Vancouver; I don't care about other places. Stints in Ottawa and Whitehorse, and travel throughout the U.S. and Latin America left me convinced that this city of water and mountains was where I belonged. What family there was, was here. Moving was not an option. It felt like limbo. For the first time in a dozen years I wasn't working on a project, amassing facts and details and getting immersed in a story. I wasn't doing ... anything.

Money, for now, was not a problem. There was cash in the bank, bonds, mutual funds, a buy-out from the CBC. Wendy lit a cigarette, put down her beer, looked at me and said: "You know, you've talked about your adoption and finding your mom for as long as I've known you.

You're never going to be whole until you find her and answer those questions."

Like reaching an arm to a drowning person, Wendy's observation offered something to grab on to. Primarily, a reason to stop gazing longingly at sharp kitchen implements and get something done: a project to which time and energy could be devoted. And, indeed, the subject of adoption and all that entailed — aloneness, differentness, abandonment, an unknown heritage — had crept into conversations with Wendy and countless other friends. She was right. After years devoted to telling other peoples' stories, it was time to learn my own.

So the search begins for roots, and answers to the fundamental question of my life: why was I born? Why was I given away? Who knows the answers? My mother, presumably. Who was my mother? And likely my father. Who was my father? It is hard not to think of them in the past tense — was, instead of is — because their direct involvement in my life ended at my birth 33 years ago. A third of a century has come and gone since I came and they went. Where were they, and where are they now? "Are" they, in fact, at all? I don't even know what verb tense to use when talking about them.

Before setting out to find answers to my questions, I've got to face the tragedy that almost every child faces — the death of a parent — even before knowing who that parent was. Or is. Am I prepared to accept the fact that they might be dead, and no longer findable? It is a fact of life, death. I am comfortable with facts. And this search can be started like any other journalistic endeavor, coldly, academically, the same approach taken when faced with untangling a maze of corporate interconnections or political crime. Gather the facts and keep emotion out of it, as much as possible under the circumstances. Better yet, pretend it is just another story. I'm accustomed to finding and telling stories. This story just happens to be about me.

Stop pretending. This isn't just another story. This is the biggest story of my life. This *is* the story of my life. But emotions can be put aside, to be dealt with later. Hell, if I don't find anything, or anyone, I won't have to deal with emotions at all, except the emotion of sadness about failure. And there have been enough failures to now; another one would be just one more.

But underlying my quest for "just-the-facts, mom," is a personal wish to touch someone who has my genes. To hold the hand of kin. To know what it's like looking into the eyes of someone connected to you by bonds of blood. To have that feeling, maybe even just once, of context. That's part of what's missing, too. It's not just facts. The facts are inextricably entwined with real live human beings, at least people who were once alive. I am not looking only for data. I am looking to belong, bearing in mind that the people I might find are not necessarily people I want to know.

Where to begin? At the beginning, asking the question: what needs to be found? Answer: the identities of the people who were, are, my mother and father. It's like solving a puzzle based on a few clues. And no, you can't buy a vowel from Vanna.

If I've learned anything about investigating, it's that the old acronym KISS applies: Keep It Simple, Stupid. Try the easiest route first. If that fails, then move on to something more elaborate. But don't try the hard tricks before you've exhausted the simple stuff.

So far, the registry of Parent Finders hadn't helped. No one had joined the registry looking for someone born on my birthday. And the non-identifying information sheet indicated that neither parent had links to my home town of Vancouver, so a newspaper classified ad probably wouldn't help. Most newspaper readers have likely skimmed past the sections in question, usually listed under "Personals" or "Information Wanted" or "People Finders," the kind of ad that reads "Male born Vancouver Sept. 10, 1955, seeks birth parents. Call 555-1212." Or "Birth mom seeks son born Vancouver Sept. 10, 1955." They tend to be placed on or around birthdays, and can be surprisingly and inexpensively successful. In this case, however, there was no way of knowing in which newspaper to place an ad. This project would have to grow from the ground up.

The first step, then, was to figure out what was already known, what clues were already in place. The biggest, and oldest: the original adoption order, thankfully retained by Fred and Ann Ouston among the family papers. They didn't know if the document would ever be useful to anyone, but unlike too many adoptive parents, they were prepared to give their adopted children whatever help they could if they chose to search.

In B.C., adoption orders contained the original name of the adoptee up until the mid-1960s, when the name was replaced with a number. My name, as I had always known, was originally Paul Anthony Griffin. No one knew where that name came from.

The adoption order also contained the name of the judge who ruled in favor of the adoption, a woman identified as secretary with the Children's Aid Society of the Catholic Archdiocese of Vancouver, and the lawyer who acted for Fred and Ann Ouston. The order also mentioned a report from the Superintendent of Child Welfare, and "a declaration of the mother of the said infant." There was no further mention of the contents of either statement.

The order was stamped with the seal of the Supreme Court of British Columbia, signed by the judge, and entered into the records book July 20, 1957 as Vol. 10, Folio 140.

Attached was another document which said that "this court doth order and adjudge that the Consent to this adoption of the mother of the above-named infant, Paul Anthony Griffin, who was born at St. Paul's Hospital in the City of Vancouver, in the Province of British Columbia, on the 10th day of September, A.D. 1955, BE AND IS HEREBY DISPENSED WITH." There was no elaboration or explanation.

That's what the adoption order said.

What it didn't say was who my parents were. But it did offer some hints. There were names: the lawyer, the judge, the church secretary. Names to pursue, to track down through the years and find them in their homes and learn the truth.

Trouble was, there was no indication that any of them knew much of anything more than was listed in this adoption order from 30 years ago. And even if they were found, and were still alive, the prohibitions against revealing any information about adoption still existed. They were bound by order of church and state to maintain their secrets, even if their secrets were about me.

I've read and heard far too many adoption-reunion stories about people who have spent years pursuing a name, be it social worker or nurse or lawyer, only to find at the end of the search that the person was either dead, forgetful or tight-lipped. There was no point wasting time on these people. Not now. Not at first. At first, do what's easiest.

And, very importantly, do not assume. Some teachers

break the word down, advising students that if they assume "You make an ASS-of-U-and-ME." Responding to assumptions or jumping to conclusions is a good way to waste time in any research project. If you are armed with only limited information, however, you must deduce — that is, to infer, or draw a conclusion. Figure out what is the most likely outcome of a set of facts, and proceed from there.

For now, the adoption order likely offered one huge clue: my name. Paul Anthony Griffin. Someone must have given that name to the baby boy, and that someone was likely my mother. And, in all likelihood, the name she gave her baby was her own. Griffin. Probably her surname. She was unmarried in 1955, it appeared, so Griffin would likely be her maiden name. That is, if she had gotten married in the intervening years. The subject of my search was probably a woman who was once, and no longer, named Griffin.

Which meant that Griffin would likely not be the father's name. Or maybe it was. Or maybe the mother had lied about her name, plucking one out of the air and applying it to her bastard child, knowing that the name would be changed upon adoption anyway so her secret would be safe. Maybe Griffin wasn't a clue at all, but a red herring. But it was all I had from the adoption order, and appeared the best route to start. If the name was a concoction, or smokescreen, I'd likely never find either parent

The second, and final, piece of paper to work with was the non-identifying information sheet. Useless, as far as I was concerned, were the conclusions and observations drawn by the social worker who drafted the letter. Kissing off the young mother as "not a very communicative person" who "tended to keep to herself" didn't help, hinder or further any search for whoever that person was 33 years later. Almost as useless was the physical information about her:

weights fluctuate during the years; hair color changes. A woman described as an attractive petite brunette in 1955 could well have matured into a plump blonde a third of a century later.

Likewise for the father. He'd likely not change in height, but weight comes and goes, and hair mostly goes. That he had a "medium complexion" and "round features" (whatever they were) was not a lot to go on. Looking for individuals matching the descriptions contained in the non-identifying information would prove fruitless. I guess that's why it's called non-identifying.

More promising, however, was the notation that dad, whoever he was, had been a member of the U.S. Air Force, stationed on the Atlantic Ocean island of Newfoundland and working as a "radar mechanic." That juicy little collection of factoids seemed the likeliest place to start my search. The reason: as people travel through life, joining organizations, they leave a trail like a slug's — shimmering, barely visible, but easy to trace once you realize how to follow it. The U.S. Veterans' Administration keeps extensive records for military pensions and medical services. As well, as a Canadian I knew that Newfoundland had joined Confederation in 1949, giving up its status as a dependency of Britain. There couldn't have been that many U.S. servicemen stationed in Canada's newest and eastern-most province in the couple of years leading up to my birth.

The first stop was the main branch of the Vancouver Public Library to gather what information was immediately available on Newfoundland playing home to U.S. military personnel. Within an hour, history books explained that more than 50,000 U.S. servicemen had worked on military installations leased to the U.S. following the Second World War.

Fifty thousand men. That's an awful lot of men.

True, the non-identifying information gave a birthdate of March 29, 1932, and an occupation of radar mechanic. But a quick skim of military occupations listed no mention of anyone having ever worked as a radar mechanic. And while the VA likely keeps computerized information and can call up a serviceman's identity by birthdate, it struck me that the military superpower to the south likely protected the identities of its fighting men. U.S. military personnel had served around the world, and there was no doubt that they left a lot of babies in their wake. It was unlikely that the U.S. government would be willing to assist one of those army orphans in tracking down his or her wayward father. If other avenues proved unsuccessful I could try advertising in publications aimed at U.S. Air Force veterans, or scour the membership lists of legions and other veteran's clubs, but that could take months, maybe years, and without a name to look for, it seemed like a lot of work.

Keep It Simple, Stupid. The veteran clue looked promising, but they say looks can be deceiving, and clichés become clichés because of the truth they contain.

While at the library I pulled the telephone books for Newfoundland, that being the province where my mother and father were said to have met. A half hour of browsing through phone books unearthed hosts of Griffins scattered throughout Newfoundland. I started jotting down the various Griffins and their phone numbers.

But once they were all in my notebook, I realized I was wasting my time and effort. Sure, I could phone all the people named Griffin and ask them if they knew of any female family member born three weeks after New Year's Day, 1934. But anyone called would likely want to know why someone was phoning long distance from Vancouver looking for a 55-year-old relative. The chances were good that young Miss Griffin had kept the fact of her pregnancy a secret from her family and friends. The fact that the first child was born in Nova Scotia and the second clear across the country in Vancouver attested to the possibility that she had not wanted the comfort of her family around the delivery table.

If she had taken such heroic measures back then to preserve the shameful secret of my birth, her son would not expose her secret to her relatives all these years later. Ann Ouston hadn't raised her son to be an idiot, or an uncaring boor. No, this would take more finesse than blundering about on the telephone lines.

Information about the mother was sketchy: birthdate, dead father, many siblings, she met my father in Newfoundland, they had a kid in Nova Scotia. At the time of my birth, she was 21.

And I realized I had already wasted a day at the library chasing military background.

There are two more catch phrases associated with how to do, and not do, an investigation or research project. Both have to do with animals.

First, if you hear hoof beats, don't think immediately of giraffes. It's probably just horses.

Second, at the start of a search, don't jump on your horse and gallop wildly off in all directions.

Keep it simple, keep it focused, keep it easy.

The first time I read the sheet of non-identifying information, I was nineteen years old, an unskilled laborer and high school dropout. Now, after a dozen years of honing some skills in the craft of investigative journalism, the key to all this seemed right in front of my face. In 1974 I had lacked the wherewithal to spot it. Now it screamed.

So far, these were the facts:

❑ There had been a mother.

❑ She was born on January 21, 1934.

❑ Because we knew she was born, there must have been a birth certificate, or a registration of a live birth. Every province and state demands that type of registration.

❑ She met my father in Newfoundland. That meeting must have taken place before their first child was born in Nova Scotia. It was likely, then, that this unknown mother of mine had at one time lived in Newfoundland. And because people didn't travel to and from the rocky fishing province back then, it was likely she was born in Newfoundland.

❑ Her last name was likely Griffin.

And there was even more to go on.

❑ Her father died at the age of 62 in 1952.

❑ He must have been born — and hence, have a registered birth.

❑ Because he was dead, there must have been a death certificate.

❑ Few people moved to, or from, Newfoundland in the first half of this century. It was likely he was born there, and died near the place of his birth.

❑ His daughter's maiden name was likely Griffin. That must have been his name, too.

In Canada, the provincial departments of Vital Statistics retain records of births and deaths. That information is freely available upon request, as long as the file clerk handling the request doesn't think it's touchy or controversial. Spending money on a long-distance phone call might tip one's hand. It was less conspicuous, and cheaper, to make the requests by mail. And in those letters to Vital Statistics in Newfoundland, I never mentioned the A word

— adoption. Instead, my letters said only that I was researching genealogical information about my family. One letter asked for records of a birth certificate for a female named Griffin who was born January 21, 1934. It would have been simple enough for a file clerk to walk to the right cabinet, open the door, and determine whether such information existed.

But a birth certificate alone would be of little value. I already knew that my mother had been born: I was proof of that. True, the birth certificate would likely give a first name for this woman whose last name might be Griffin. But all this time later it was likely she had gotten married, maybe married and divorced and married again. And until recently, society forced all women to maintain the damnable practice of changing their names to their husband's. Damnable to any searcher trying to trace the movements of someone he didn't know.

The request for the death certificate of a male named Griffin who died in 1952 would seem a little looser and perhaps harder for a file clerk to complete. Several males of that surname would have died that year. But the non-identifying sheet said he was 62 in 1952. Depending on his birthdate, that meant he was born in 1889 or 1890. Surely it would be simple enough for a file clerk to zip through the records to find a man named Griffin, born 1889-90, died 1952.

The letters were sent, and the wait began.

It didn't last long.

Within two weeks, an envelope from the Newfoundland department of Vital Statistics arrived at my home. Inside was a photocopy of the registration of birth of a woman named Maureen Jerome Griffin.

Sex: Female
Date: January 21, 1934

Place: Corner Brook
Father: John Joseph Griffin
Mother: Mary Ann Griffin

Maureen Jerome? Was I holding the proof of the birth of my mother?

It mentioned a place: Corner Brook. The name evoked vague memories of a harbour city, a provincial capital, but little else. Was my mother from Corner Brook?

I picked up the phone and dialed directory assistance, area code 709.

"Hello, operator. Do you have a listing for a Griffin, first name Maureen?" It feels strange to say out loud for the first time the name of the person who might be my mother.

"No. There's no such listing. Not for that first name."

Oh.

It should not be a surprise. She may be moved, dead, married with a different name. The birth information is added to the pathetic little stack of documents and I wait.

Less than a week later, a photocopy of a death certificate arrives.

Name of deceased: John Griffin
Age: 62
Sex: Male
Date of Death: April 23, 1952
Place of Death: Corner Brook
Marital status: Married

There is nothing in the certificate to say if this is John Griffin who was father of Maureen Griffin. Nothing tying the two together, or me with them. But now I have a date and a place — Corner Brook, and April 23, 1952. Of the journalistic Five Ws, that's the "where" and "when." And we know the who: John Griffin. And the what: he died.

What is unknown is the "why." And, frankly, I'm not that interested in how he died. He may have been my grandfather, but he was dead years before I was born. But his death could be the key that unlocks the next door. In a town as small as Corner Brook, the death of a citizen would surely rate a mention in the local newspaper, at least in the obituary columns. And obits, as they're known in the newspaper trade, usually mention the names of those left behind to mourn.

In Vancouver, I was not mourning. And I was not about to spend time waiting on the Canadian postal service. Directory assistance gave me a phone number for the Corner Brook newspaper, and the local library. I called the library. Newspapers usually maintain back issues and good records in their library, or "morgue," but newspapers are profit-making enterprises, usually short-staffed, and they don't have time to search through musty yellowing newsprint for every caller who wishes to know an arcane fact. Libraries, however, are full of helpful librarians whose job and passion it is to uncover information for the public. Most libraries retain back issues of their local papers, in heavy bound copies or on microfilm. As a reporter, I've developed an overwhelming respect for libraries and the people who work in them. As an adoptee, I hoped that respect would sound in my voice as I phoned across the country, asking the librarian who answered to look in the microfilm for the city paper published immediately after April 23, 1952, looking for an obituary for a John Griffin.

The woman who answered the call took the request for the obit, and the offer to call me collect with anything she might find.

She called later that day and read the obituary over the phone.

"John J. Griffin passed away at the Western Memorial Hospital at 4:30 Tuesday morning. John J. Griffin, in his 62nd year."

The obit went on, recounting John's profession, his travels, and listed, among those left to mourn, a daughter, Maureen, at home, along with a couple of sons and a handful of other daughters.

Maureen. He had a daughter called Maureen. A daughter called Maureen, and daughters called many other names, and sons.

This was proof there once was a woman named Maureen, whose last name was Griffin, whose father's name was John. And John was dead.

What it was not was proof that Maureen Griffin was my mother. The woman who was my mother may have adopted a friend's name as a cover story to protect her own identity. She may have lied, as a scared young pregnant person, and vanished, returning to her own name, leaving her son a trail grown cold with deceit.

But this is what I had to go on.

The paper trail led directly to a human trail. Instead of accessing documents and not disturbing suspicions, I would now have to talk with a real, live human being, and ask where Maureen is today.

The next move would be tricky. If this Maureen Griffin truly was the woman I was looking for, she still might have secrets to protect. This was no time to go blundering about, phoning indiscreetly.

Who best to call? Probably those least connected to Maureen — wives of the brothers, related to her only through marriage instead of blood. They would be less likely to demand a reason for divulging Maureen's whereabouts than her sisters. Still, it was risky; I might have to bail out, dump the receiver down, finish the search here, rather than exposing my mother's secret.

The directory assistance operator had numbers for Griffins with the same first names as John's sons. I would phone during working hours in Newfoundland (four and a half hours ahead of Vancouver, Newfoundland occupies a time zone unique in the world) hoping that the husbands would be at work, and their wives would answer the phone.

That might work:

- ❐ if these are the right Griffins, sons of John;
- ❐ if Maureen's whereabouts are in fact known;
- ❐ if Maureen is, in fact, still alive,
- ❐ and if the small-town wives don't get suspicious about receiving a phone call out of the blue from a stranger who does not identify himself but instead asks if they know where Maureen lives these days, with a tossed-off comment about how I lost track of her a long time ago.

I was prepared to lie, saying I was an old friend of hers. I was prepared to learn she was long dead, victim of disease or the drug addiction into which she fell after giving birth to an illegitimate child. I was prepared to hang up if the supposed sister-in-law got too nosy.

I was not prepared to hear a woman's voice saying, "Oh yes! I guess her kids are all grown up now. Haven't seen her for the longest time. She's Mo Landon now. I've got her address right here, wait a minute. Here it is."

And there it was. She was alive, apparently, and well, and living in Durango, Colorado. And she'd had children, according to this sister-in-law who didn't know she was talking to her own nephew.

That is, this was all true if the information my mother provided the social worker was correct and not a phony name or identity.

The woman's voice on the line finishes reading out the address, and then asks: "Would you like a phone number for her?"

I try not to sound anxious. "Yes, please," nonchalantly. I am sweating, hoping the woman on the phone cannot hear my fear.

"Thanks for your help," I hear myself say quickly. "Bye now," and I hang up before she has a chance to ask my identity. Small-town woman, small-town virtues and values, more trusting than in the big cities. Maybe the man on the phone sounded like a nice young man to her. She certainly had no way of knowing the man on the phone was her nephew, and that he was talking to a relative, albeit through marriage and not blood, for the first time.

In journalism, there is a sensation that washes over a researcher at the point in the hunt for the story when you know that you've finally got the goods. Call it the "gotcha" point. Whether it's a carefully crafted question during an interview that catches the bad guy, or the discovery of a document which acts as the smoking gun to prove the theory, the gotcha point is when you know you've got the story, that it's real, and the hunt is finished.

I have never known my mother, but this is what I am thinking about this unknown person: Gotcha!

Three

I have an address for my mother, then. Her first name, and her address and her phone number. She's alive, and she got married, apparently, and she has a permanent address. She has a life, then, this woman who is maybe my mother. She has a life, and a name, and a town, and U.S. Bell has her listed.

A young male voice answers the phone with a rapid-fire delivery that I can't quite comprehend. I am likely speaking to a brother, a half-brother. The voice of my blood. "She's not here," the young voice says. "She'll be home at eight."

It is a very long wait. Eight-oh-one, her time, dialing the number. I've plugged my tape recorder into the phone. I want to keep the words.

Is this the former Maureen Griffin of Newfoundland?

Laughter, and she says yes.

I'm calling from Vancouver. My name, at birth, was Paul Anthony Griffin. I was born on September 10th, 1955, at St. Paul's Hospital. I realize this is a long time later, but as near as I can tell, you're my mother.

(There. I've said it. If the woman who was my mother

borrowed a name, then this woman is not her. If this woman is my mother, but doesn't want to be, or doesn't want to know me, she can now hang up. She can tell me to go away. She can demand that I never phone again. She can say no, you've got the wrong person.)

She says nothing.

Silence.

Then: "Where are you?"

In Vancouver.

"You've gotta give me a minute."

Is this a good time to talk, or a bad time?

A sigh. "Go ahead."

I realize this is coming like a ton of bricks, and it was a very long time ago. You were a child.

"I know." Sob. "Paul." Sob.

(She hasn't denied me. She could have said I had the wrong person, that she wasn't my mother. She could have hung up. She could have told me to go away and never bother her again. She could have done all those things. But she hasn't. She calls me Paul. My mother is crying on the phone. I must think of words to say, words to say so she won't hang up.)

A very long time has passed, I tell her. I've grown up. I'm fairly happy.

"Are you?"

Yes. Life has turned out pretty well for me.

"What do you do?"

I'm a journalist, in Vancouver. (You know, I've never thought of this: she might have read one of my newspaper stories, or even seen me on a television news broadcast.) You may have seen some of my stories on NBC or CNN.

"Oh Paul." Another sob. "D'you know, I was, thought this would happen someday. I don't know how to handle it right now. You ... give me some time?"

(It's been 33 years. A third of a century. A lifetime. My lifetime. She can have all the time she wants.)

"Paul. I do love you."

My throat catches. Oh God, I sigh, thank you for that.

"Where are your folks?"

Mom here, father died when I was twelve. Two sisters, both adopted.

"How did you find me?"

I start to explain, but when I reach the point where my adoptive parents always made sure that I knew my original name, she whispered: "Paul Anthony. I have a son, a son named Paul. I have a son named Roger, a son named Daniel, and a daughter named Lori.

"Oh, I don't know what to do. I've never told anybody about this. I never told my husband. He doesn't know."

I expected that might be a possibility. So much has changed between then and now.

"I know. I know."

You were a Catholic kid at a time when people didn't talk about kids becoming parents. You must have been scared. (Think of words to say. I don't have a script. This isn't a performance. This isn't a rehearsal, or a fantasy. This is real. I am talking with my mother. My mother is real. She is frightened, and I don't know what to say.)

"Well, I had a mother who would not accept this, you know, and I had to run away. And she doesn't even know. Nobody knows, only me. My sisters, my brothers, my family, my husband, my children, only me. And I lived there and, you know, was in limbo. Paul."

Another sob, and a silence. (If this was a television interview, these silent lapses would be the nugget that held the viewer in thrall. A good reporter never interrupts pregnant silence with questions. Get the emotion on tape. Record it. Let the tears tell the story. But this isn't a television interview. This isn't someone else's life I'm dissecting for a paycheque. This is my life, and this woman crying on the phone is my mother.)

I say: It's a secret you've kept for a very long time.

"I had no one to tell it to. You know, I had a family that would never accept it, none of them.

"Hello Paul." (But she wasn't talking to me. Her son, Paul, the other Paul, had walked in the door.)

Then it was time to talk in code, me talking on my side, her listening.

(I need the words. Thank God for television. The delivery may not be perfect, but I think I can say the right things to push the right buttons to make it all right. I haven't practiced this, but words come.)

It's not my right to ask you to tell people now, I tell her. It's not my right to ask you to tell your husband. Or your kids. It is a marvelous feeling hearing your voice, knowing that you're alive, that you're here. That you did make a life for yourself. I have no right to impinge on the life that you've made ... but I'd like to. (There. I've said it. I want something. I want something of you. I am a part of you, and I want.) Just to see you in person, and to talk in person. You owe me nothing. You gave me birth, and I thank you for that. You gave me life. I wound up with a very loving family.

"Um. Can I have a number?"

(She can't talk now. I know that. She wants my phone number. Maybe she will call. I can hear her fumble for a pen, and I can see in my mind a blank piece of paper. When you write a phone number down, you always want to have a name to go on top. She doesn't know my name. She called me Paul. But Paul is not my name, in my world.)

My name now, and it's been ever since I can recall, is Rick, and my last name is Ouston. O-U-S-T-O-N.

"Rick." She tastes the flavor of the name of her son who was Paul.

Will you phone me, or should I phone you?

More of the code.

"Tomorrow."

Thank you.

"I love you."

Bless your heart.

"I love you."

Bye.

Hanging up, numb. My mind usually works fairly quickly. But I can find nothing to focus on. Just one fact: I have just talked with my mother. My mother. I have a mother. Her name is Maureen. She lives in Durango.

She says she loves me.

My mother loves me.

Oh God.

My adoptive sister Sharon is also looking for her parents. She cries on the phone when I tell her. I phone friends, and tell them. Repeating the story enough times so that it becomes true.

What happens if she doesn't phone? She sounded nervous, defensive. Her first words, the first words my mother said to her son, were "Where are you?" Instinctive self-preservation, like putting your hands in front of your face if you think you're going to fall. Was I close enough, physically, to threaten her with my presence? Was I on her front door, or at the phone booth outside the Durango Shell station? Was I going to ruin her family? She had a family. That was good. She hadn't become a junkie on the streets of Vancouver. She hadn't died from drugs, or by her own hand. All the scenarios I was ready for. I had prepared myself for what might have been. Now there was no way to know what might come next.

I have a mother. Her name is Maureen. She says she will phone me tomorrow. I wonder if she will. I pour the first of several scotches. Without too many drinks, I will never sleep, wondering if my mother might phone.

She does. At 8:10 a.m.

A distant voice of a telephone operator. Will you accept a collect call from Mo?

"Rick? It's me."

(No name. No title. Not Maureen. Not mom. Me. Me was good enough for me. She called me Rick. Overnight I had changed names. Overnight, in her mind, I had become a person with a name. A name, and a reality to deal with.)

She's sorry about calling collect, but her husband would see the phone bill and wonder who she was calling in Vancouver.

"I didn't sleep at all last night. Well, I did ... I had a thousand dreams. My stomach is in knots. What do you need to know?"

(What do I need to know? What do I need? This woman who is a stranger and who is my mother has thought about my phone call, and knows that the man who is her son has a need. A need for what, she doesn't know. Implicit in her tone of voice is the suggestion that this might be it, the only time we'll ever speak. One phone call then, then another, then nothing. If that's how it is to be, fine; I'll make the best of it. If she can't talk to me, then maybe my father can. I don't want to push her, into hanging up the phone and cutting off contact. The thought of forcing her to recall the man who fathered me is dangerous. But if I don't ask, I may never know.)

What can you tell me about my father?

His name was Donald. He loved hockey. He was three years older, and she loved him and would do anything for him.

(Don't push it. Back off. The seed of memory is now planted. We'll get back to him later.)

The records say you had a daughter in 1954. Is that my sister?

"Oh," she says. "The Nova Scotia incident." It was in Sydney. She was given up to the Catholic Family Aid. No one knew. She went back home to Donald.

She offers no name for the "Nova Scotia incident." No birthdate, no birth name. She wonders if I'd try to find my sister, and I say I'd like to. But I can't push on this point. Like interviewing a reluctant witness for a news story, I must be calm, I must be patient. I must be content to get what I get. This might be the last time we ever talk.

She'd put the Nova Scotia incident behind her. She went back to Donald. And I came along. (She does not use the word "pregnant," that dirty little word with connotations of shame and terror. I "came along." In 1955, people came along. In 1955, good girls didn't have sex with their boyfriends. The word "pregnant" wasn't used on television till the mid-sixties. Pregnant was a dirty word.)

But when she had me, she loved me, she says. She came to Vancouver. She lived in the Vancouver suburb of South Burnaby. She worked. She doesn't say at what.

"I was all alone. No radio, no television. Nothing. I went through hell."

(She mouths clichés, TV soap opera dialogue. She is not sophisticated.)

What can you tell me about my father?

She had lied to the Catholic Charities officers. "I didn't want anyone to know." Had told a story about a U.S. serviceman. It had been Donald. Twice. He was a local boy. He told her to come back. They could work it out.

(I am glad that years weren't wasted trying to track down the phantom radar mechanic with round features who was invented to hide the shame.)

She went to Glace Bay and got a job. Her mother is now 95, and she says things that lead Mo to believe that she knows. (That she knows about me. The dirty secret of my birth.)

Donald is dead. She found out when she went back to Corner Brook to visit her family some years ago, after the husband of one of her sisters had died.

"It's ironic. My brother-in-law is buried two stones away from Donald. My sister said, 'Oh yeah, there's Donald O'Connor. He died in a car accident. The first one to die on the Trans-Canada Highway. You used to go with him, didn't you?' I said yes."

Within about twelve hours, I have found a mother and lost a father. I had always thought I'd find my father, this unknown American, and have a drink. And talk. I'd seen the bar a lot of times. It was crowded, and dark, and noisy with the sounds of many people. I never heard my father speak, and never saw his face, but that was him in the fantasy. Now he is dead. Tears for another dead father will have to wait.

She thinks he died three or four years, maybe five, after she went away. She doesn't know the year. I say "Oh." (Maybe she's lying. Maybe he really is alive, but she just doesn't want me to find him, in fear that her family might get wind of the secret. But the "ironic" part of the closeness of the tombstones rings too true for it to be a lie. I want it to be a lie. My father is dead. Twice in one lifetime my father has died. And she tosses it off, a fact best left forgotten, like my birth. His death, my birth.)

"You wouldn't just come down here and show up here, would you?"

(She is alive, and afraid. She fears the knock on the door. The sound of the knock on the door is a sound she has heard in the night. In the night, she has felt her husband leave her, and has felt her life again alone. She dreads the knock on the door.)

I say: Not if you don't want me to, no. I wouldn't do that to you.

"Are you smoking?" she asks. "I had a cigarette last night. The first one in a long time."

I tell her about my marriage, my divorce. We were two young kids, too young for marriage. About going to school, about becoming a journalist.

She is proud that I went to school. Proud that I became a journalist. She is glad for me.

(She is afraid of me.)

"I went to South Dakota to visit a sister, and I met Roger. He was a college boy. And after three days, he told me he loved me. I said 'Sure, the whole world loves me.' Then, after a few weeks, he said he still loved me. We got married. It'll be 32 years this August. I love him more every day. But he's a man of few words. I don't know what he'd say if I told him. He might say, 'You go your way, I'll go mine.' I don't know. Help me, Rick. What should I do?"

(She has called me Rick, again. She has asked for help. My mother has asked for help. Is she truly seeking my advice, my opinion? Or is this a trick of words, to get me to accept that the problem is just unsolvable and better left dropped? I don't know. I don't know this woman. I don't know her husband. I don't know what kind of help I can give. I don't know how these people would react. This is 1989. Attitudes have changed. But in the conservative small towns and small-town minds of Corner Brook, Newfoundland, and Durango, Colorado, it's not 1989. Not to people who think of love-children and illegitimate kids and shame of having sex with your boyfriend. Would the small-town minds of Durango accept the fact of the bastard son of Maureen Landon?)

"I hear them talk, I know what they say about people. I hear them talk like that and I say to myself, 'If you only knew.' I know what they think. My oldest son, he's very straightforward, very straight. He thinks people should be honest. How can I tell him?"

(This son is my blood. A half-brother. Disgusting term. Like "half-breed." A pejorative from the past. A term as outdated as bastard and illegitimate. Disgusting to think that my brother could be a pig-headed oaf who would think ill of his mother, my mother, for having sex with her boyfriend. My brother. I have a brother, kind of.)

I say: If I was your son, and I am, I would be proud of you for having the honesty to tell me.

(I think: I am trying to talk my mother into revealing her rancid secret to her family and risk losing 32 years of time and love.)

She says: "If you did come down here, would you bring up the Nova Scotia incident? They might be able to handle one. Two ... two ... "

(This Maureen who is my mother fears that her family will think her a slut. A whore. My mother, the whore. My mother, the easy lay. Could her sons think that? Of their mother? Of my mother?)

I say: Not if you wouldn't want me to, no.

I think: I will find this girl, this sister of mine who is a woman. I will. Even though my mother doesn't want me to in fear of her family tattooing her with a scarlet letter. It is my right. It is her right, this incident who is a person. Who is my sister. I will find her. My mother and I have known each other for twelve hours and a few minutes and already I am keeping secrets from her. In my silence, I am lying to this unknown woman. We have talked for twenty minutes, and I listen to her voice and I can't see a face.

Then she says: "You know, what I want to do is to see you, to have my arms stretched wide and ..." Tears. Hers. Mine. Simple words, but powerful imagery when shared between a mother and son who are strangers.

I cry too.

Tell me about yourself, she says.

I am five-eight, I tan easily, brown hair, eyes are small.

Your nose, she says. Do you have a Roman nose?

I don't know what a Roman nose is. But I tell her that my nose is about half a size too large for my face.

She laughs. She is five-foot-one, she says. A pause, and she says, sadly, that she's heavy. That happens, she says. About 130 pounds. Her hair is dark, she says, then corrects herself. Was dark. (I try to visualize her face from the voice and I can't. Has she dyed her hair blonde as a 52-year-old small-town gas-station wife, or has it just gone grey? I've acquired a shock of grey in the front of my head but because I can't see her face I don't think of asking her.)

My mother says she can see herself and Donald, my dead father — in me. Her mind can see my face. My mind cannot see hers.

Is there a photograph of you two together? I ask. The answer is no. (This is not a surprise, although I am sad. It is not a surprise that a young woman who had lived a lie for 33 years after my birth would destroy the evidence lest questions arise.) But she says that a family portrait was taken recently. Would I like one?

(Would I like to see my mother's face? Would I like to see the faces of brothers that I will never know? Would I like to see people who look like me? Blood of my blood.

I can see the Landon boys in my mind, uncomfortable young men unaccustomed to wearing ties. Angular, tanned faces. Roger is a pump jockey. Overweight. I can see the boys and the girl — her name is Lori. She is my sister — but I cannot see my mother's face.) She writes my address, and says she will mail the photo.

I want to see my mother. I want to talk to you, in person, I tell her. I offer her an airline ticket to Vancouver, but she declines. "We don't have much money, Rick, and he'd wonder where I got it from." I can't go to Durango and meet her surreptitiously, because Durango is a small town, and people in small towns talk. "You go out one afternoon and the next day eleven people tell you they saw you yesterday."

I say I don't want to make her keep another secret from her family. (More soothing words. More lies from a son to his mother. I want her to do whatever it takes for us to see each other, and if it takes a lie then lie, dammit. Your life has been a lie, in part, for 34 years, across a continent, in two nations, with a son and a daughter. Yes, I want you to lie, if you must. Lie for me. Lie for your son. But I don't tell my mother this.)

She will feel her family out on the matter. "Maybe I'll tell them I saw this in a movie, and ask them what they think. That might do it, do you think?"

(An unsophisticated approach, and I find the small-town minds amusing. But she has begun to think of lies to tell, of ways to do it. She might. In twelve hours and a few minutes she has come a long way, this unknown mother named Maureen.)

She says she needs some time. She will contact me when she's ready.

I say: I will wait.

(I think: I will wait. For now.)

Four

*I*t is times like this when one is grateful for a wide circle of friends and acquaintances. Not so much for support, as for an audience. So much has happened in a few short hours: mother lost, mother found; father lost, father lost now forever; a lead on an unknown sister who has a brother she doesn't know about. By nature and profession a story teller, I feel a powerful need to tell this story of discovery to close friends, then not-so-close friends, then acquaintances, co-workers and colleagues, anyone who will listen.

Helen Slinger comes to the house, dog and daughter in tow. She sits on the back porch and listens to every word, detail and nuance, a blow-by-blow account that only a trained journalist can expect another journalist to remember and recount. We listen to the tape recording of the telephone call. She knows her friend needs to tell his story, needs to make it real by repeating it, needs to give the story to someone, to share it, to work out his feelings and emotions and the facts to make sure he's not missing anything, hasn't made too many mistakes.

When Helen leaves, I phone other friends. Then, tired

of repeating the story on the phone, I visit the Vancouver Press Club and, after ordering a pint, tell the story to the barmaid. She listens intently. I've known her for a decade, and have rambled on about the news stories *du jour* throughout that time, but never has she been as receptive as this.

"I had a son," she says. "I gave him up for adoption." She tallies the years. He's almost a man now. If he's still alive. He's almost old enough to go searching on his own. She has not registered with any of the agencies. It is something she thinks she should do. It is something that terrifies her.

"I don't want to interfere in his life," she says, not thinking that he may register — might already have registered — and be waiting for word from his mother. She was a child herself when she gave birth and life, and when she succumbed to the pressures of family and society to give the child away to someone better equipped to raise him, she gave up any rights to that life. That is the reasoning she accepted then; maybe now, she says, it is time to change her mind.

Another woman in the bar has been listening to our conversation. "I had a daughter," she says. The same story. The women listen as I recount phone calls and searching tips and I realize they are not listening to my story. They have cast me in the role of the children they gave up years earlier. They are hearing my words but placing them in the mouths of their own children, trying them on for size, wondering what it would be like to hear the words from the children, now nearly adults, who were their children.

Who are their children still.

Perhaps they will join a registry, sign up for Parent Finders in various countries. They are afraid. What would it be like if they found their children? What would it be like if they didn't? Maybe he'd hate me, one mother thinks. Maybe he'd love you, the other mother says. How about the adoptive parents, how would they feel? Wouldn't they think I was interfering?

I have already phoned Ann Ouston and told her. "Oh I'm so glad!" she said. "We'd always thought, Fred and I, that you kids might want to do that." We have the relationship we have, my mother Ann and I, built on the experiences and personalities that make up the people we are. In our case, we're not close, but the discovery of this other mother is not going to alter whatever bonds there are between us. That relationship already exists, the same as any adoptee and adoptive parent, the same as any child and any parent. They love or detest each other somewhere on a sliding scale; the introduction of a birth parent later in life is not going to change that relationship.

The women at the bar hear the words, but in their minds they remember a pregnancy so long ago, and visualize the person that pregnancy became. And they still feel the loss of the child they've never known.

As a man, sitting on a bar stool, I am surprised to realize that I'm feeling like someone's child. Having spent much of my time proving to the world that I was grown and adult and independent, after two phone calls with a woman I've never known it strikes me that from now on I will play another role: that of the child of Maureen, the child she's never known. Until now.

That means that the solitary pursuit of wondering about, then searching for, a story of a life, now has been transformed into a story of two lives: a mother and her son. This is no longer just about the subject most people find dearest: "Me." Now this is about her, too. And us.

I wonder what will happen next.

It happens too soon.

Just a day passes before the phone rings.

"Rick, it's me. Your mom. I love you."

(She's phoned direct, not collect.)

"I told Roger about you last night. He's right here. Do you want to talk to him?" Then, off to the side of the phone receiver, muffled, "Roger, he's on the phone. Here." The sound of a telephone being passed from one hand to another.

(I wish this wasn't happening. What do I say to this man? What do I mean to this man? Does he feel cuckolded, proprietary and angry that someone else had his woman? Is he supportive of his wife, the woman he has professed to love for more than 32 years? Is he magnanimous, an eighties-kind-o'-guy who understands the old ways weren't necessarily the best ways? What does he want from me? He's not my father. What do I want from him? Nothing. Mom, Mo, whatever I'm supposed to call you, I wish you weren't doing this to me.)

Waiting, for a man's voice on the telephone. Waiting, wondering what to say. Waiting, hearing nothing.

Then, the voice of Mo on the phone. "I guess he doesn't want to talk to you right now. I'd better go. Good bye. I love you." The click of a phone line gone dead.

*T*his is what I want to know: what the hell was that all about? Why has she told him? Because she felt she had to? Because she thought he'd be supportive? Because she felt not to was a lie? Why? Apparently he's not responding the way she thought he would. From the sound on the phone line, the telephone was passed to Roger the husband, then back again to Mo. That could only mean he'd declined the offer to speak with the child of his wife. Offer? Or was it a demand? Or a plea? Had there been tears then, last night, shared between wife and husband? Hugs of reassurance? Arguments and bitter words, or whispers of encouragement? Have husband and wife grown closer together, or is my looking into the past already ruining the life my mother created for herself? No, this is no longer just about me. This is about her and hers and us and ours, and because of me she might not have any of hers anymore.

Two days ago I didn't know who she was, this unknown mother of mine. This day, I wonder if not knowing would have been better. It is too late for would-have-beens. Whatever blunders have occurred, hers, mine, have occurred. Now we await the fallout, this mother and her son who are strangers.

Late that night, she calls again. Collect.

"Rick," she says. "I'm scared."

She'd told Roger the truth about her first-born son. She thought he'd be supportive. He grew quiet, asking for no details, saying nothing. She felt relieved that he did not attack her, no angry words. Elated, she'd phoned her son. But as well as no angry words from Roger, there were no words at all. He sits in his study, his chin resting on a fist, staring straight ahead, saying nothing.

"I don't know what he's going to do," says Mo. "He says we've been living a lie all these years. I don't know if he's thinking of leaving or what. Rick, help me. What should I do?"

A mother, in tears, seeking advice from a son she doesn't know. A son, on the phone, fearing he's wrecked his mother's life. Again. I do not know this man. I do not know this woman. I don't know what relationship they have, or don't have, how strong or fragile their bonds of trust. Mo has obviously felt the bonds were stronger or deeper than her husband does. Truly, I don't know what to say.

What I want to say is: You've really screwed up. And you're making me feel guilty. It's not fair.

But it is fair. Because I am guilty. Guilty of re-opening old wounds. Maybe adoption is for the best. Accepting that what's done is done and being "as if born to" means letting the past remain in the past.

I say none of this. She is married to a man who is being a boor. Who is being a man's man, manly in that quiet way that men from his era and birthplace are supposed to be. A man of few words, Mo had called him. A man's gotta do what a man's gotta do. And this man feels he's gotta be an asshole. Maybe his manhood is threatened. His wife, his woman, had sex with someone else. Of course this had happened long before the two even knew each other. But that's just a fact, and manly men don't let facts stand in the way of their manhood being hurt. Roger must be thinking of someone else having had his woman. An affair. She's screwed around on him. He's been kicked in the balls by the truth and his heart hurts. This is what he's thought of his wife's confession: So, what's it mean to me? This is what I think: So, Mo, you sure can pick 'em, eh? Donald knocks you up and you go back to him and he knocks you up again and then doesn't come out to Vancouver and marry you, then you marry Roger who is being real intelligent and caring and compassionate. Good choice in men, mom.

(Then: okay, Rick. Stop blaming. Maybe I'm being too hard on Roger. I don't know the man, and he is of an era when men thought that way. And if that's the way he thinks, I probably don't ever want to know him. This is your mother on the phone. You need a game plan, words of advice to your mother, helpful insights to save the day and make yourself look like a good and wise man. I don't have a game plan.)

I say: "I don't know what to say."

She says: "I'm scared. But I'm glad you found me. I don't blame you. I'm glad. But I'm scared. I don't know what's going to happen. I love you."

She hangs up the phone.

I want to beat up the man who married my mother. To pound his head into a wall and shove my finger into his chest and say: Listen, pal. I'm here. You better accept that and start giving your wife some support.

That fantasy finished, I wonder what there is I really can do. Roger refused to speak with his wife's secret. He doesn't want to hear from me. That means a letter to him is probably too forward. He'd think it an invasion, feel threatened that I was entering his space, disrupting the life he thought he had.

If he won't read a letter, maybe he'd read a newspaper story that presents the issue with some fairness. If the story appears in the public eye as fact, and not just as one man's word against another man's hurt, maybe the husband of my mother will accept the reality of my reality without confusing that with a loss of love for his wife. Words in newspapers usually carry a certain authority. If I write it and send it to him, maybe he'll change his mind. If he sees himself on a newspaper page, maybe he'll see the light. At the very least, other men might see themselves in the words. As it turns out, Father's Day is just a few days away. I write a freelance editorial for the local morning daily paper, which is published Sunday, June 18, under a headline reading: "Father's Day Tells My Story."

"The man I called father is dead," the story began. "It happened a long time ago, his death, so the words don't hurt so much now. But this year, Father's Day holds a special meaning, because in the last few weeks I've learned of another couple of fathers, men whose lives are inextricably tied to mine. One of them is my father. The other is the father of my mother's children."

I went on to tell about my adoption by Ann and Fred Ouston, about missing the touch of kin folk, and about finding Mo and her life and times. I wrote about her reticence in telling her husband, the final blurting out of the long-suppressed story, and about the husband's reaction.

> She doesn't blame me, she says. And I, honestly, cannot blame myself. To know the facts of my life, we feel, is my right. She hopes that the father who is married to my mother can accept this.
>
> I hope so, too.
>
> So, on this Father's Day, I have no father to speak of, but I offer a message to the man who married my mother. This is a day for celebrating life, for celebrating the fathers who participate in that miracle. The woman who is my mother, the woman who is your wife, gave me life. Please don't think ill of her for that.

It was weeks before Mo phoned again. She had asked me not to send her anything by mail — Roger picked up the mail each morning and he'd be suspicious — so I had been unable to send the clipping to her. When she phoned again, mid-summer by now, late at night and collect "just to say I love you," I asked if there was a way to send the article. "Please don't," she said. "It's been six weeks now and he's barely said anything to me."

As many as a million people saw the story in the newspaper. The one man it was directed at didn't.

*A*ll the television sets at the airport in Denver, Colorado, are tuned to CNN. It is the height of the Gulf War, Iraq versus the world. Canadian soldiers fight alongside military personnel from the U.S., the former Soviet Union, old enemies now allies massed against Saddam Hussein, bent on rescuing Kuwait and the oil that country contains.

I am changing flights, catching the third connection of the day. Vancouver to Seattle, Seattle to Denver, Denver to the city where my mother has recently moved. After two years of secret phone calls, she's finally going to risk it — a meeting with her son. It will be brief, clandestine, just an hour or so this night, perhaps an hour or so the next day, then I'll fly back home. Roger mustn't know. It must be kept a secret.

Mo regrets telling him the truth of her past. The two have barely spoken about it since. Roger says flatly: "I don't accept it." What he finds unacceptable is truth, fact. He refuses to accept the pain of his wife, the reality of her son. An ostrich's-eye view of the human condition, but a view all too prevalent among men of Roger's age and standing. I can understand his way of thinking, I think. It stems from the time when men were not supposed to have emotion, a time when the man's word was law. Father knows best. If we don't talk about it, it will go away. All the "its," like spousal assaults, like incest, like alcoholism, like teenage pregnancies, like homosexuality, like anything you wouldn't want the neighbors to know. When the subject of adoption comes up on the television, on talk shows or movies of the week, Mo changes the station, usually while crying.

She is happy, she says, that I found her. She is afraid, she says, of her family. Of losing Roger, of losing them all. What contact she has with her son is sporadic. Only she can phone, and then only at night, when her husband is in bed, and collect, so the transgression doesn't show up on the phone bill. If I'm home when she calls we can talk. If I'm not, the answering machine clicks on and she cannot leave a message, so her son doesn't know the number of times his mother has called to him in the night without success.

Mo has grown to trust the man who is her son. He hasn't shown up at her front door, demanding attention or affection or money. He has stayed away and waited, and a rhythm has developed between mother and son. She has stopped, finally, asking: "Do you hate me? Do you hate me for abandoning you?" No, her son has answered again and again and again. There is no hate. I understand the times and attitudes of the day. Attitudes that Roger has carried over to this day. No, I don't hate you, her son says. "I love you," says Mo. I love you, too, her son says.

But he lies. In truth, he feels no love for a woman he has never met. Not a love of passion or commitment or unconditional respect or admiration. Not even a love of being loved. In the phone calls, late at night, whispered on her end, I feel there is no good reason to tell her: I don't love you. It would only be hurtful. She would think her son was saying "I hate you," and that wouldn't be fair, or accurate. As hate is an intense emotion, love is too. I have felt romantic love. I have felt bonds of what I suppose is love for friends. But I don't know enough about this woman who is my mother to feel love, or hate, or much of anything. I can empathize with her plight. I can sympathize. I rejoice in the fact that it is done now, that

I no longer must wonder about this unknown woman who bore the child that was me. Psychologically, it's called effecting closure — completing that which was not done. Intellectually, the facts add up to what is supposed to be a happy ending: orphan and mother reunited at last. And indeed I feel truly happy about what has transpired to now. But when my mother says she loves me and I say I love her, it is still a lie. I don't know her. I don't know if you can love someone you don't know.

If you can, I want to know. I want to feel it. I want to see what might be possible.

I want.

And finally, she wants too. To see her son. To hold him. Again. It had only been the once, at the hospital, that she held her tiny baby boy. Once, before the nurses and the nuns took him away. Now, after talking with her son on the telephone a score of times, she has agreed to meet him. More than a year has passed since our first conversation. To the world, we have aged, but to each other we are still tiny baby and scared young mother.

A room is booked at the local Holiday Inn, waiting for me in the city where she now lives. The Denver Airport is busy, full of people and luggage and noise and CNN. No one at the airport knows that the man wearing a grey flannel suit and carrying a shoulder bag is going to visit his mother for the first time in his life. I feel like a little kid, afraid of the unknown, going somewhere for the first time. Chronologically, I am a man. Fully grown, hair already turning grey. Outside, my tie is tied, my wallet full of credit cards capable of booking rooms and renting cars and paying for airport drinks. Outside, I look like a man. Inside, I feel like someone's son. A boy. A very small boy.

The other men walking around me at this airport are real men. Tall and confident, knowing what they're doing and where they're going. I feel like I've shrunk during the first two legs of this journey. The other men are tall, as tall as my father Fred was tall when I was an elementary school kid looking straight up to see his face. The men here are tall and I am short, too short, shrinking quickly, surrounded by men twice my height and I am in full panic now.

This is not a nightmare or hallucination. The men here truly are taller than other men, and this man. Members of the Denver Nuggets professional basketball team are returning home from a road trip. Our flight arrivals have coincided. They hustle past, men paid millions for being taller and faster than normal men. I stop and laugh, in the hallway of the Denver airport, then work my way to the third and final flight of the day.

Tonight, I meet my mother.

*P*acing. From the bed to the bathroom and back and forth and back again. A feeling of being trapped inside four walls with the standard bed, desk, table and chairs, and toilet sanitized for your convenience, which means in the words of a long-forgotten comedian, "No one has used the toilet since this piece of paper was placed over the seat. She'll be here at eight. That's the time we set, weeks earlier. Eight o'clock, her time. The flight arrived at four and I am pacing, pacing, pacing. I want a drink. But the smell of booze on my breath is not the first thing my mother should note about her son. I want to drink, but I can't, so I pace.

And pace some more. I am wearing a suit and shirt and tie, and it would be nice to loosen the tie and shuck the suit jacket, but I want to look good for my mom. I don't want my mom to think her son's a bum. The local newspaper contains nothing of interest. The sections are dissected, lying on the bed. The local news on the television tells of fires and crimes and what went wrong today. The reporters and editors who cover this community know nothing of the grand passion play that's unfolding in their town tonight. Tonight, a son meets his mother for the first time. It would make an interesting feature story, for a reporter to write, for readers to read between visits to the bathroom and the fridge, during commercial breaks on the television. An interesting tale of mother and orphan, reunited. That's the word the reporter would use: reunion. But the word implies that the parties to the reunion were once consciously united. As with most adoptees, this pacing man who wants a drink has no memory of ever having been with his unknown mother, of ever sharing the same air. With no memory of a union to begin with, there can be no *re*union for me. This will be a first in my conscious memory.

For her, I don't know. We haven't talked about how much time, if any, mother and son spent together all those years ago in Vancouver. I don't know if she'll view it as a reunion, or union, or just something that she must undergo to assuage the demands of a man who was once her son and who is now a stranger.

I pace the floor of the Holiday Inn awaiting the arrival of a woman I don't know. It feels, well, seedy, like preparing for an affair in a no-tell motel, or paying for a visiting prostitute picked at random from the Yellow Pages section for "escort agencies," the kind that promise relaxation to the travelling businessman at his office or hotel. Partly it has to do with the secrecy of it all. Keeping it behind closed doors, me telling no one, she lying to her husband to escape for a couple of hours with a man who is not her husband. With a man who is her son. I wait for the knock on the door that will indicate that the wait is over.

The knock comes.

I open the door and there stands a woman, shorter than most, mid-fifties, overweight, blonde, the kind of middle-aged woman you see in hordes at department store sales and never give a second glance. This is my mother? This is my mother. I don't know what to do. Shake hands? That's pretty formal. Hug? A bit forward. She looks up into my face and smiles and takes the initiative, reaching arms wide and clasping her son to her chest. She's a mom. She knows how to hug. She's learned how to hug her children during their growing-up years. Now she hugs her first-born son. I hug back.

We feel the touch of each other. Alone, together, in a hotel room, mother and son, touching.

There is only one thought in my brain: I am touching my mother. This is no longer a fantasy. No longer a dim longing. No longer something that I needed to do. I am doing it. I am hugging my mother. Time is running fast on the hugometre. Is it time to break the embrace? If it's too soon, she may feel slighted, rejected, dismissed. If it's too long, she may feel monopolized, controlled, that her son is grasping for a mommy. Again, she takes the initiative, lets go, takes a pace back, looks into my face. I look back, into her face. There are similarities. She has my squinty little eyes. The same set to her jaw. The same nose I see while shaving.

She looks a little bit like Popeye the Sailor Man, strong-jawed with a half-smile smirk. She looks like me. It is weird to see a woman with my face, to see a feminine version of myself. This is what people see at family reunions, in the faces of their brothers and sisters and aunts and uncles, in the faces of people whose faces are shaped by shared genes. That is what the unadopted see. That is what the adopted never see. Never, until now.

"Don't you go crying now," she says, smiling, eyes welling. I think I'm supposed to cry. At least squeeze out a tear or two. Isn't that how it's done in the movies, tears from mother and orphaned son reunited? It feels like I could, if I wanted to, cry. Just a little. I remove my glasses and wipe my eyes so my mother can see me do it, can see that her son at least felt like crying.

It strikes me: this woman and I have just met, and already I'm play-acting for her. Putting myself in a role. Putting on a performance. I don't know what to do in front of a mother. Never have. Never have had to. Acting comes naturally, role playing, and if there is a dance to be danced at this event, I'll dance it.

"I love you, my darling," she says, and we hug again.

Small talk now, of flights and travel, of stories told to husbands to allow time for this illicit meeting. She has come to the hotel with a friend, a friend who picked her up at home. The husband thinks she is going to a meeting of local business people. The friend thinks she's dropping in to see a relative, a nephew from Canada. The friend is waiting. We don't have much time. Talk of airline food and war in the Persian Gulf, keep the words flowing so we can look at each other. Mostly so I can look at her. She has sons, three of them. She has seen their faces, at birth, during childhood, maturing, faces growing into adolescence and adulthood. For her, seeing a blood relative is not a new thing. For me, it is novel. It is hard not to stare.

We have so much to talk about. Thirty-five years. So much has happened. We have so little to talk about. We are strangers, speaking of lives which are unknown to each other.

Now I take the initiative. Preparing for the trip, I've

assembled a photo album, Ricky Grows Up, my life in pictures. Perhaps my mother would like to see the childhood she never saw. Perhaps it will mean something to her. Perhaps it will at least give us something to talk about.

The first photos, the earliest, black and white, show a small boy around three years old, dressed in overalls, in a cage full of white rabbits. Apparently the small boy is me. I have no memories of visiting the bunnies, or of the farm where they were kept.

The next page, photos of Ann and Fred Ouston. Fred in his hardhat, standing outside a long forgotten construction project. He is smiling. He looks like Everyman. Ann, in a posed shot by a portrait studio years after her husband's death, a smiling grey-haired lady in glasses. Fred and Ann have Page Two prominence because I want Mo to understand I'm not looking for a mommy. I have a mommy. This is her, on the page in the photo album. That's the message I hope Page Two sends.

Then there are school pictures, young Ricky in Grade 1, Grade 6, a golden sticker of Jesus attached to a card addressed "To Ricky Ouston, for the best all around boy in Gr. 5," signed by a nun. (See, mommy, I was a good boy. I don't want a mommy. But I want to impress this mommy. Partially for myself, ego-boosting; partially for her: it was okay to leave your son in an orphanage. He turned out all right. Is she getting these messages, or just seeing photos? What is she thinking?)

She turns the page. Photos of her son, fully grown now, posing with the woman who would become his wife, then his ex-wife. We hold each other, we hug, we kiss. (Yes, I've talked about rights for gays and lesbians and an end to homophobia on the telephone. But in case you were wondering why I'm not married, mother, see, here's proof. I'm not a fag. I am, though, a hypocrite. Or maybe just an opportunist. What message does she get? I don't know.)

Rick graduating from college, dressed in gown, clutching diploma. Shots of family and friends, Ouston family, in-law family and ex-family. Nieces and nephews, the kids of my sisters, the family that her son knows. (These are the faces that your son sees when he thinks of family. Now included will be your face.)

Press passes, a page full, media identification with mug shots showing my face with various lengths of beard and sans beard. (Oh by the way, they also show that your son the big-deal reporter covers popes and princes and politicians. Yes, your son walks with kings. Pretty smart guy, eh? Enough about me, what do you think about me?)

Rick on TV, Rick interviewing people on TV, a photo from Rick's wedding, Rick's cat Lou.

She turns the pages, listens to my words of explanation, who's who and why, but the expression on her face is vague. There are no squeals of joy. I thought maybe she'd be entranced by the opportunity to see what she'd missed, that she'd revel in having access to a past denied. Instead she seems faintly bored.

Have you ever been forced to flip through the pages of a photo album of a friend or relative, the mundane collections of events which are milestones for them but mean nothing to you? Home movies and videos and slides of places and people who mean nothing to you and who will never mean anything to you? Mostly, it is a courtesy, seeing the pictures through, listening to the tale, waiting for the end so you can do or say something meaningful. That is what I've inflicted on my mother. My life, and the pictures of that life, is a life foreign to her, foreign from hers. It is the life of a stranger. The stranger who is her son.

She re-opens the album to the page with Rick in Grade 8. Opening her purse, she takes out a plastic window wallet, stuffed with photographs. Shuffling, sorting, she stops and hands a photograph to me. It is the face of a teenage boy, maybe thirteen or so. "That's Paul," she says. "He looks like you, like you looked, doesn't he?"

There is a faint resemblance, something about the face, maybe the mouth. (I don't want to see pictures of the other Paul. I want to learn about my mother, Paul's mother. Both Pauls. For God's sake don't show me pictures of your children, the children that you kept. Please don't! But I cannot say this.)

The pictures start coming. Sons and daughter at various ages, their lives and times. Occupations and who did what in school. Hobbies and passions. Nieces and nephews and granddaughters and names, so many names, one is married to another and each of the photos has names and I don't want to hear the names. I don't want to know about these people because I will never know these people. These people don't know me. If the secret remains a secret, they never will. They are my half-brothers and half-sister. They are strangers. They are my family, the family that will never be.

My mother is telling me about herself through these pictures. These are the pictures of her life, a life that revolves around the children she's had and the family she's made. She doesn't seem to realize that by concentrating on the photographs of her children, her unsecret children, she is again excluding me from her life.

(All right mom, I want to say, I get the picture. I understand you have a life, and there's no room for me in that life. At least no room for me in public. I understand that you treasure your family above anything else. I understand that you can't risk losing that family by accommodating the son you wish you never had. Do you understand that with every photograph you pull from that plastic wallet you're causing me to wish I wasn't here? I wish I could say this, but I can't, and I wait for the pictures to end.)

Finally they do. She tells me that she and Roger go about their business now as if nothing ever happened, as if I had never happened. They don't talk about it, about me. Every now and then, though, she sees Roger watching her, and she doesn't know what to think. It doesn't feel the same, not like how it felt between them before Roger learned her secret. They don't talk about it, but Roger gives her this look.

It's the same kind of look Mo's mother gives her when she visits back home in Newfoundland. The mother is 97 years old now, but from the looks she gives and the comments she makes, my mother thinks that her mother knows about her daughter's secret. Or at least suspects something. She's never said anything, but she gives those looks.

It was her mother, she says, who forced her to leave home so young. Mo had been the apple of her father's eye, his favorite daughter, but when he died at the age of 62, only her mother remained, and her mother didn't like her.

"She was abusive, Rick, she really was. I couldn't take it anymore. I had to leave."

In 1955, pregnant with me, she waited for Donald to come and marry her. She loved him. She loves him still. He never came. She went back home for a while, visited a sister, got married, had a life.

"I didn't want to leave you, Rick. You understand that, don't you? There was just nothing else I could have done. My mother would not have accepted it. Never. Never in a million years. Do you hate me?" She is crying.

Once again she hears her son say no, I don't hate you. Once again she hears the words, but this is the first time she's seen her son say the words. She needs to see, and hear, and know it's all right. After all these years.

(She is seeking absolution, just like in a Catholic confessional. My mother wants her son to absolve her of her sins, the sin of having been an unmarried mother. I am no priest. No one calls me Father. I am just a son, but if my mother needs her son to absolve her of guilt, real or perceived, then so be it. She needs, and I can give. This is the first time in her life she has talked about her son, except for a few minutes with Roger. That supreme act of womanhood, giving birth, creating life, that precious gift that women have and men do not, has been shrouded all these years, all my lifetime, behind a mist of regret and tears and shame and fear that her baby would hate his mother. That her baby must hate, because abandoning a baby is the most hateful crime a mother could commit, in the eyes of a mother. My mother.)

"I don't hate you. You're my mother, for God's sake."

"I love you, Rick."

"I love you, too." Again, the lie. I don't feel love, even after hugging and touching my mother. What I do feel is sorrow, sorrow for her pain. I am feeling sorry for my mother. That's not what I came here for. I came here for me. I tracked this woman down for me. I wanted to touch, and to see. I wanted for me. Now, in less than an hour between mother and son, another agenda makes itself felt. My mother has needs, too. This meeting is for her, too. If she needs to see me say I love you, then I'll say it. Is that in itself an act of love? Or a little white lie for which a priest would demand three Hail Marys in penance? My mother has lied, about herself, about me, since my birth. If someone has to share the burden of lies, then let it be her son.

"Rick, about the other one, you wouldn't go looking for her, would you?"

The other one. She can still not say the words — my

daughter, my first-born, my first pregnancy, the other child I left behind. She refers to the baby she bore as an object, not even in the third person. Not as a person at all.

"The first time, I hated what was happening. I hated what was happening to me, and I hated what I had to do. I hated what happened. I hate her.

"But the second time, with you, I loved you. I thought I'd be able to keep you, so when I was pregnant I grew to love you. Then I had you, and, and, and I had to leave you. But I loved you. You know that, don't you?"

"Yes, I know."

"You wouldn't find her, would you?"

"I don't know."

(Again, I am lying to my mother. I've already spent time trying to locate this unknown sister. So far the governmental registry in Nova Scotia is a bust, and even efforts to find her adoptive name and the names of her adoptive parents through the baptismal records have gone nowhere. Maybe now, maybe now I will drop it. I've found my mother, and met her. That's a lot, and maybe that's enough. There is no way for "the other one" to know that I exist. But I can't honestly say that I won't continue seeking my sister, her daughter. Or is it honest to say that, right now, sitting at a table with my mother is enough? For now. I don't really know the answer.)

"I don't know."

It is time for her to leave. If she stays any longer her husband could grow suspicious. Her friend is still waiting downstairs in the lobby. We hug, again. I walk with her out the door, through the hallway, down the stairs to the lobby where the friend is waiting. We walk arm in arm, my mother and I. There are introductions. I am her nephew, from Canada. We are lying to my mother's friend. The lies come easily, shared between mother and son. She might be able to pop by tomorrow, she says, she might not. A final hug, and she walks away.

The hotel gives coupons good for five free drinks at the hotel lounge. I order a double scotch and a beer, and after the scotch is finished, another. So this is how it feels to meet your mother for the first time. I am not a different person than I was. The man who flew into this city today is the same man who sits at the bar tonight. There has been no change, no alteration.

But that which was undone is now done. Like normal people, I have a mother; I have seen her; I have touched her. Just like normal people.

*I*t already feels a tad anticlimactic in the Holiday Inn the next morning. Okay, I've met my mother. That which was undone, is now done. Now what? I guess that's it. There should be a crescendo of strings in the background music, cheering crowds, TV appearances. I should be taller, wiser, changed somehow, a different man. Instead, the image in the mirror is the same one I saw yesterday. Just one thing has changed. A mother and son, separated at birth, are no longer separate. There is a chance we'll never see each other again. But when we think of each other, when I think of the woman who was my mother, I can see a face, feel a touch, remember a room. When she thinks of the son she gave up at birth, she can see a man who does not hate her.

Tiny things, really, in a couple of lives and lifetimes. A couple of extra memories, adding up to much more than a one-hour meeting.

The flight back home leaves at three. There is time for a generic hotel breakfast of tasteless food, a game show on TV.

The phone rings and it is Mo. "I can be over in five minutes." She is back.

She has more photos. More pictures of her sons and daughter and granddaughters. Photos of Paul, the second Paul, growing up. "He looks like you," she says, smiling.

I hate the pictures. I try not to drum my fingers against the hotel table, fighting down the impatience that threatens to ring with sarcasm in my voice as more photographs are passed from mother to son. The mother is proud of the son who bears the name of her first son. She loves her baby. She dotes on Paul, the other Paul.

There should be no jealousy of this person who is my half-brother and who is a stranger. I don't know him; I don't know our mother. How can I feel jealous of people I don't know? As the photographs slide across the table, mother to son, the son isn't sure how he feels. Angry, perhaps. My mother is trying to reinforce the reality that it's impossible to have closer ties between us. (Yes, mother, I understand your plight. No, mother, I don't want a mommy anyway. Stop being so blatantly obvious. Is there no subtlety in our genes?) Maybe just boredom, feigning interest in faces of people who I don't know, who I will never know, who don't know me, who, to protect the secret, must never know me. Finally the stack of photos runs out and we can talk of other things.

"When I went home last night, I started thinking. Maybe I can tell Lori about you, about what happened. She'd understand. She'd be supportive, I think. The boys I'm not sure of. I've heard them talk. But Lori would probably support me. And Roger loves her; she's his baby. If she told Roger what to do, he'd do it. But I don't know. I don't know."

You need to talk to someone, her son says. This is an awful lot to keep bottled up. You've got to find someone to share this with. (Good God, I sound like Ann Landers.

Wake up and smell the coffee, hon. Speak with your minister. Get some counselling. Here we are, separated by lifetimes, your baby boy advising you on life skills. Role reversal, big time. Isn't it the mom who's supposed to have the answers? But the memory of me is locked tight in her heart and her head, stuck in the same place she put it 35 years ago. A realization: I am almost twice as old as Mo was when she had me. Whatever perspective I have on all this is based on a lifetime of thought. For Mo, it has been locked away, untouched. She sees her son through the eyes of the child she was, not the middle-aged woman she is.)

We talk about women's rights — how views of unwed mothers have changed — and that leads to talk of rights and politics, minority rights and racism.

"I'm not racist," says Mo. "Some people around here, boy, are they ever. Not me, though. Although I've got to tell you, if I go to a restaurant and find out it's run by Vietnamese, I just get up and leave. They killed so many of our boys."

(Of course it's not as if the people of that country invited the U.S. to drop bombs on their heads and burn their babies. Don't do it, Rick. Don't fight the Vietnam War in the Holiday Inn with your mother. She's a Yankee, you are not. Her logic may not coincide with yours, but let it be.)

"And Indians, you know how *they* are ..."

(Of course you're not a racist. You just sound like one.)

"There aren't too many blacks around here. That's why the crime levels are so low ..."

(My mother, the bigot.)

It is time to go. I am glad it is time to go. I want to leave, to get away from my mother. A hug, a kiss, a final two-way I-love-you, then I'm in a taxi headed for the airport.

I don't much like my mother, I realize. It hurts to think that thought. She is naive. Small-minded. Her politics are a product of geography, at least in part. Any chance at further education dashed by the fruits of her womb. Spending an adulthood isolated in small-town USA, she has the world view of June Cleaver, extending all the way to her children and no further.

This does not make her a bad person, that she does not measure up to the standards demanded by her unknown son. It just means that I haven't seen much to like. I realize that the endless display of photographs was not some clandestine plot to chase me away. Those photos are merely what she knows. She has shared what she is with her son in the only way she knows how. She is a mom, Everymom, dedicated to the raising of children, living her life through their lives. That she is Everymom with a secret past is irrelevant to the life she has chosen. She looks for all the world like most other moms approaching 60. To see her would not trigger suspicions that she may have fled her childhood home to give birth to a secret child. Twice.

If you saw her on the street, she would blend in with all the other aging mothers of the world. Some are wise, some are not, mine is who she is. That I don't much like who she is, is, I suppose, something all children of all parents decide for themselves at some point in their lives. Today I have been given the chance to decide this for myself, having met and touched and talked.

If I had admired her, or saw something during our meeting that smacked of mental kinship with the person I am, it would have been a bonus. As it is, we have met, and the sense of absence, of something left to do, is gone. It is replaced not so much by a feeling of accomplishment as by an absence of absence.

We shared a bond, in that hotel room, being mother

and son together for the first time. She is proud of her son. He is not an axe murderer or a drug addict. She must be relieved, at least, to know that the baby she left behind bears no ill will toward his mother, is not psychologically ruined by the way he was raised. She must trust, by now, that her secret son is not going to barge into her life, demanding a place in her family, a seat at the kitchen table.

This meeting, this rectification of something left undone, was something I wanted for myself. I hadn't thought about what my mother wanted. During the long taxi ride to the airport, it becomes obvious that this has been a selfish, self-centred quest until now. Now we have met. Now we feel like "we" — two people, two sets of wishes. Two lives, hers and mine. I had wanted something for me. Without realizing it, without planning for it, I have given something to someone else: peace of mind. To give. Giving to someone who needs to get. Is that just simple human consideration? Or is it love?

These last two days may be the last time we ever see each other, I think. That's perhaps not such a bad thing. She doesn't need the stress of sneaking behind the backs of her family. I don't need a mommy, particularly one whose philosophies differ so much from my own. We were separated, now united. She needed to be told her son loved her; she has that now and always will. She might tell a daughter, or a son. There may be secret meetings or phone calls in the future. But for now, for the present, we have done what we have done, and that can never be undone.

*A*t the airport, a voice booms through the public address system.

"Paging Mister Rick Ouston. Will Mister Rick Ouston please report to the security gate. Will Mister Rick Ouston please report to the security gate."

The only person who knows I'm here is sister Sharon. It is our routine for me to tell her where I can be found when I'm travelling, in case of a family emergency. Our mother is past 73, pretty spry for her age, but we know that lifetimes are not eternal. Sharon has never had to call me during vacations or business trips. Now, walking toward the airport security gate, I think: Why now?

The old man wearing a cap with a badge points around the corner. I look for a phone but instead, there stands Mo. She is smiling.

"I just wanted to see you again before you left," she says, spreading her arms. We hug.

"Your plane leaves soon, I know that. I just wanted to tell you I love you, my darling."

We hug again, kisses on the cheek, smiles. A stupid grin crosses my face and I can't help it. She is being all the mother she can be to the son she cannot have.

"I've gotta go."

"I know."

And a mother watches her son walk down an airport hallway. He stops before turning the corner, turns around, still smiling, waves. She smiles back, waves. Neither of us can share our joy with anyone at the airport. To do that would be to expose the secret. It is good enough to know what we know. We have shared ourselves with each other.

Five

_M_y adoptive sister Lorraine left her motorcycle club, the Grim Reapers, soon after marrying her childhood sweetheart Dave. The two had gone together since Lorraine was thirteen; they got married when Lorraine was just out of high school and just a little bit pregnant. We stayed in touch, barely, with me paying the occasional visit to Lorraine and Dave's home on Vancouver Island to play uncle with her three daughters. I did not make a very good uncle, showing up just once in a while and not knowing what to say to prepubescent children. Lorraine ran her home with an open-door policy, always a spare room for stray friends eager for a couple of days out of the city, so the uncomfortable uncle was never made to feel dramatically out of place. And with a revolving circle of friends dropping in and out, the fridge was always full of perogies and cabbage rolls and other gut-fillers that could be microwaved whenever hunger struck. A pool table in the rec room and a house full of kids and friends added up to an ideal, if mundane, nuclear family. And long before Roseanne showed up on TV, Lorraine was always ready with a smart-ass wise-crack to wake people up, like turning a radio announcer's notation that the song you just heard was A Good Man is Hard to Find into "Yeah, and a Hard Man is Good to Find," sneaking in the malapropism when it's least expected and most welcome. Despite the mortgage load and responsibilities of children, it looked at least stable to this divorced thirty-something who had neither home nor kids nor the promise of either. Each time, on the ferry ride back to Vancouver, I felt a tad envious of my adoptive sister who at least had a family of her own making to call her own.

She asked me to come to the hospital for the birth of her third child, her third caesarean section. The first two had been rough births; doctors suggested she should stop at two. But the first two were daughters, and Lorraine and Dave hoped for a son, so they tried one more time. When the nurses wheeled the pale Lorraine from the delivery room, she cried when she saw Dave, and held his hand and said through tears: "I'm sorry. I'm sorry, Dave." It was a girl, another, and it would be the last. Probably the drugs, nurses said, were what made the mother weep bitter and angry tears over the sex of her new child. Probably, I thought. It certainly wasn't the happy time the sitcoms made childbirth out to be. It was my first pacing of a nursery floor; it too, I suspect, will be the last.

Lorraine had never tried looking for her birth parents. She'd say she was interested in finding out the circumstances behind her birth, but just never got around to doing anything about it. The surname on her birth certificate was rare — a quick search through the local phone book found just a handful of listings sharing her original last name — but Lorraine had taken no action. It was Sharon who finally phoned the names listed in the phone book. Using a cover story, she unearthed the name of Lorraine's mother. Word was passed back to the woman, who replied that she was old, that her husband was sick, that Lorraine's birth had been the result of what would have been called rape today, and that she didn't want anything to do with the child to whom she had given birth.

The woman lived just a few blocks from where the Ouston kids grew up. True, she had asked for privacy, but it would have been so easy to sit in a parked car outside her house and at least get a peek of the woman. Lorraine never got around to it. When we talked adoption, and reunion, she'd talk vaguely about how she might visit her mother one day, or catch a glimpse of her at church, but nothing ever happened. I never pushed the issue; the literature about adoption issues says some adoptees feel a need to know while others aren't troubled by the unknown.

Lorraine and I developed a rhythm over the years: small talk at my arrival, discussions of jobs and friends and how's-your-life?, then heading out to a bar to drink beer and shoot pool, sometimes with Dave, sometimes with other visitors and neighbors, often with a fellow member of Lorraine's women's pool league or curling club, sometimes just us two. It perhaps doesn't sound like much, but it was as close to brother-and-sister bonding as we got. The visits were sporadic, every couple of years or so, but it felt like something close to tradition, and at nights over a bottle of scotch we began sharing things we felt.

Things like the fact that neither of us felt close to the Ouston family, or a part of any family in particular. We admitted to each other that we were orphans and felt like it. And that when Fred Ouston died, his family died with him. The orphans he adopted became orphans again. Certainly, we had continued living together — at least until each of us was old enough to legally leave home — but sharing the same bathroom does not a family make. The Ouston family had revolved around Fred at the head of the kitchen table, making friends on the job and at church, and providing his adopted kids with a social life. When he died, Ann Ouston's spirit died too. It hurt to admit it, shared the brother and sister who weren't, but in truth we didn't really feel much at all for the Ouston family. Not hostility, or animosity, anger, or even dissatisfaction. Just, well ... nothing.

Nothing isn't much to bond the best of siblings, but it became something for us to share, and after the rest of the family went to bed, Lorraine and I would stay up, pour too many nightcaps and share the one thing we could — our differentness. What we had in common was that we had nothing in common. Like I said, it's not much, but it was all we had, and letting go of that was to let go of everything.

So that's why we were sitting in a bar on Vancouver Island in the summer of 1991. Lorraine had the day off, I'd come over for a few days of trying to play uncle, and the two of us had sneaked away from the family for a couple hours of yacking, maybe to play some pool.

The barmaid brought us pints of beer, we lit cigarettes and asked the usual so-how's-it-goin'-eh?

"My life is falling apart," said Lorraine.

This is not the standard response. And she's not smiling. This is not a joke. Well, either she's having an affair, or Dave is, or one of the kids has developed a drug habit. I'm so happy to be here.

"What's wrong?" I venture.

Says Lorraine: "I'm a homosexual in a heterosexual world." And she stops, flat. Turns her head away from mine, places hands on the armrests of the chair to get up and walk away, to let this sink into the brain of what passes for her brother. My arm reaches for hers, to stop her in her chair.

I remember: Dave and Lorraine, barely teenagers, necking in the basement, Lorraine telling me, maybe nine years old, "Don't tell Mom." A white gown and a church wedding; Dave selling his 650cc Triumph to pay for the rings. Walking to the bus stop with my sister, her purple skirt past her knees, Lorraine walking and rolling up the waist band so that, by the time we reached the bus stop, the skirt rode well above the knee and onto the thigh, which was apt for those miniskirted days but which Ann thought made Lorraine look like a hussy. Always it was Lorraine-and-Dave, uttered in one breath, one thought. Lorraine-and-Dave. Lorraine-and-Dave. Now it is to be: Lorraine-and-women? My sister the dyke?

She's not kidding.

I say: "Are you sure?"

She nods. Her face shines with sweat. There are tears in her eyes.

"How long have you known?"

And out it pours. She's always known. Her first crush was on a nun in Grade 1 at Saint Andrew's Catholic elementary school. But she knew that was wrong. Women weren't with women. Women were with men. Anything different was a schoolyard insult — "Lesbo! Faggot! Homo!" — and a sin. The church said so. She had a boyfriend because that's what you did. She got married, pregnant. Pregnant again. Because that's what you did. But all the while she had these feelings, powerful feelings, too powerful to ignore. She'd told Dave about them and he said to forget it, and they didn't talk about it again. There had been affairs, a couple, short-lived, with family friends, married women. The husbands had no idea. Life was a lie. Not that she didn't love Dave. She did, she does, oh so terribly much. But it's not the same, not the same as with a woman. It is the first time she has felt true passion. It is a feeling she does not want to abandon. It's not Dave's fault; it's my sister's fault. She doesn't want to hurt him. She doesn't want to hurt. She doesn't want to be hurt. There's no one else like her. "Oh Ricky, I feel so alone."

Married 21 years, three daughters aged twelve, sixteen and twenty, life as a masquerade, pretending to be someone she isn't. Pretending to be heterosexual, like everyone else is supposed to be. Pretending to be "normal." The pretext was becoming harder to maintain. She'd met a woman, new in town, and after too many drinks the two had fallen into each other's arms, and after they sobered up they fell back into each other's arms. The woman is lesbian. She knows it. Lorraine is too. She can't continue pretending.

Other than a couple of lovers during the years, and Dave, and now the woman in her life, Lorraine has told no one. She is 41, and one of the most basic, fundamental facts of her life — of anyone's life — her sexuality, is cloaked, hidden, closeted. She is ashamed of herself. She is scared. She is asking for help from her brother, who is a journalist, who is supposed to know stuff.

"Ricky," she says, "I don't know what to do."

Frankly, I don't know what to do either. Like most people, I hadn't given much thought, if any, to homosexuality. I knew there were people who said they were homosexual, who did sexual things with members of their own gender. Indeed, in 1983 I was the first Canadian reporter to write in the mainstream press about a new ailment known as Acquired Immune Deficiency Syndrome, a troubling phenomenon which had been affecting Haitians, homosexuals and intravenous drug users. Covering the AIDS epidemic had meant talking with — and later writing the obituaries of — a lot of gay men. But the journalistic buzz phrase of "gay lifestyle" had left me figuring that to be gay was a choice of sorts, just as a lifestyle is that which one chooses, presumably choosing that style over another. Personally, I knew that I was attracted to women. (With apologies to singing TV cowboy Roy Rogers, my first crush was on his wife Dale Evans. It would have been before first grade. Roy and Dale were on television, and there was a firmness between my legs. I didn't know what it meant, but I knew it was associated with Dale. "I could pee on her," my little-boy brain willed my mouth to say. I didn't know Ann Ouston was in the kitchen, within earshot. "You don't pee on people!" yelled Ann. Thus concluded my first lesson in sex education.)

The media were full of drag queens and gay-pride parades and pedophiles and bull dykes, to be sure. Way back in 1967, Canadian justice minister Pierre Trudeau, later to become prime minister, struck homosexuality from the criminal code, making it no longer a crime for consenting adults to do what they wanted. "The state has no place in the bedrooms of the nation," Trudeau said. I remember him saying it at the time on the radio. At the time, however, I didn't know what he meant.

There were gays and lesbians among my co-workers; gays and lesbians among the people I interviewed. And, luckily, my current neighborhood, the Commercial Drive district of Vancouver, had lately become a gathering point for the city's lesbian population. As gay men gravitated to the city's West End, full of highrises and high rents, gay women congregated in the city's east side, where housing was more in line with the fact that women still earn only about 60 per cent of the incomes of their male counterparts. Along with the second-generation Italians, first-generation Portuguese immigrants, pseudo-intellectuals, welfare recipients and wayward yuppies attracted to the neighborhood's coffee shops and European eateries, a sizable lesbian contingent staked a claim, even setting up the Vancouver Lesbian Centre a few blocks from my favorite cappuccino bar. So I knew about lesbians ... but I didn't know my sister wanted to marry one.

Lorraine needed to talk and talk we did, into the nights throughout my visit. Talked and hugged and talked some more. We spoke of being raised Catholic, about how she still believed in the church but not in the church's teachings which branded homosexuality a sin. We spoke of the lack of sex education, both at our home and in our schools, where the only talk of homosexuality occurred in whispers among kids, derisory, accompanied by sneers and insults. And we talked of Lorraine's love for her husband Dave, how she didn't want to hurt him but was sick of hurting herself. If only, she sighed, he was a woman. We spoke of a feeling of disconnection through our adoptions, untied to kin, unlike anyone else. Lorraine has lived a double whammy of despair: separate because of her adoption, further disconnected through her sexual reality.

She can't visit my lesbian neighborhood immediately because of family commitments, but we arrange for her to arrive next week.

Back at home, I visit the local feminist book store, the Book Mantel, frequented largely by a clientele of stereotypical in-your-face lesbians, many heavy-set with tattoos and butch cuts. Lorraine still spends a good half hour in the morning applying make-up and fixing her hair — "making pwetty," she called it — and I had also met lesbians over the years as attractive and well-kempt as any uptown girl. It would be interesting to see just how Lorraine might change. Later I would learn about "lipstick lesbians," and another ungrounded preconception based on clichés would fall.

Two women stand behind the counter at the book store. No one pays any attention to me. Several customers mill about the stacks of used books. More sit on stools in front of the counter. They talk among themselves, the usual melange of earnest whisperings and laughter at shared jokes. The store smells of cigarette smoke, yellowing paperbacks and coffee. I am the only male in the store. No one makes eye contact with me. This is a refuge for lesbians. I feel really stupid. Finally I catch the eye of a woman who looks as though she works here.

"Excuse me," I mumble, "I wonder if you can help me. My sister is 41 years old, married 21 years, three kids, and she's just told me she's, well, she's coming out of the closet. She lives in a small town, she doesn't know what to do, she figures there's nobody else like her. I'm hoping you might have some books that I can send to her."

The talking and the laughter ebbs. Nothing so obvious as to make me more uncomfortable — no one's staring — but enough to know that the people in the store are paying attention, and that this intruding male has pressed the right buttons.

In fact, the women are smiling. And they take charge, leading the way to the right shelf and pulling down volumes of primer material, books like *After You're Out* and *There's Something I've Been Meaning to Tell You*, books by and about gay men and lesbian women coming out of the closet, becoming truthful to themselves and their families and friends and community. Books about how and when to tell your children, and when not to tell. Books about Catholics and the closet, books about every topic that Lorraine has talked about, every thing that has made her feel all alone in the world. Literature not available in most small towns. Books that Lorraine and people like Lorraine might have found on their own if they decided to look, but when you feel there's no one else like you, you don't think there's going to be shelves full of books about you.

Bonnie Murray, one of the Book Mantel's shopkeepers,

offers to lend Lorraine a stack of material she photocopied from medical journals at the University of B.C. library when she faced her own homosexuality in 1984. The material is a few years old now, but it's a good five-pound stack of stuff, and at this point I'm just as interested in volume — keep Lorraine busy — as in value.

Bonnie tells me she was a suburban mother of two when she told her kids she was lesbian. Daughter Ailysh was nine at the time.

"I said 'What's that?'," Ailysh, now fourteen, recalls, "and she told me and I went 'Oooooo-eww!' and I wouldn't talk to her. And I told some people and word got around and I was glad to leave that school." Rocks were thrown at her house. Children were told not to play with Bonnie's kids. Parents accused the single mother of being a child molester. The family finally moved to Vancouver's inner city, and Ailysh attends high school just a block from her mother's store.

"My mother's always been the same person," Ailysh says now. "It's just now that she's more at peace with herself." Recalls Bonnie: "I thought I had totally blown it" by telling her kids. The medical journal studies in Bonnie's stack of photocopies indicated that children of lesbian mothers have a better-than-average understanding of their own sexuality — they're forced to examine themselves more closely — but Bonnie knew that telling a child young enough to be uncomfortable about any sexuality is a gamble. For Bonnie, and her daughter, the gamble paid off. I make a mental note to introduce my all-alone sister to this bookseller who was introducing me to a world to which I had paid no attention. A fat package is sent to Lorraine that night via overnight delivery, but I keep a chunk of material so I can learn myself.

*A*fter the reading, and subsequent research, I feel even stupider than I felt walking into Bonnie's bookstore that first day. Stupid, ignorant, xenophobic and really, really embarrassed that I have dismissed an entire segment of the population with a couple of newspaper catch phrases, dimly remembered schoolyard anecdotes and some truly sloppy logic.

Again and again and again, authors repeat the assertion that homosexuality is no more a "choice" or chosen "lifestyle" than is being left handed, blue eyed, short or tall, dim or brilliant. Scientists, doctors, academics, psychiatrists, counselors and just plain folks have studied the phenomenon and determined that there is a part of the human race, and always has been, that is homosexual instead of heterosexual. They argue that homosexuality is as natural for homosexuals as heterosexuality is for heterosexuals. Gay authors writing for gay readers don't even address this argument anymore. They are not out to convince the hetero segment of the population about their reality; they're writing for people who share that reality. If they were to lie, their readers would see through it. Instead, their stories and analyses contain a resonating ring of truth.

The whole experience of delving into the subject of homosexuality left me not just a bit ticked off with a society which has branded a goodly portion of its members as deviant, sick, disgusting and sinners, just because they're different. Hitler and his final-solution adherents put pink triangles on the clothes of homosexuals and sent them to the death camps. The president of an organization called P-FLAG (Parents and Friends of Lesbians and Gays), Paulette Goodman, was a Jew living in occupied Paris and she's made the connection. "I know what it's like to be in the closet," she's said.

And it's not as if people like Lorraine can take comfort and refuge in their faith. The Catholic church continues to demand conformity from its flock. As recently as 1992, U.S. bishops received a report from the Vatican entitled *Some Considerations Concerning the Response to Legislative Proposals on the Non-Discrimination of Homosexual Persons,* written by the Congregation for the Doctrine of Faith. The report stated flatly that "there is no right to homosexuality" and repeated the assertion that "homosexual orientation is an objective disorder." The Vatican says homosexual tendencies are not sinful, but homosexual behavior is — and that makes discrimination against gays fair game. States the report: "There are areas in which it is not unjust discrimination to take sexual orientation into account, for example, in the placement of children for adoption or foster care, in employment of teachers or athletic coaches and in military recruitment."

Gays and lesbians like my sister still find themselves the target of institutionalized bias. Until 1980, the official psychiatric diagnostic manual listed homosexuality as a mental disorder. A manual written by white guys, presumably all straight, who perpetuated the notion for as long as they could that anyone who wasn't like them was somehow sick. That they gave up the battle more than a decade ago doesn't mean the rest of the world has.

The New York Times quoted Naomi Lichtenstein, a social worker at the New York City gay and lesbian anti-violence project, as saying "it's as though our very existence is somehow a threat." As for the Catholic stance promoting discrimination against gay teachers and others who work with kids, it seems the church has its thinking skewed. Dr. Gregory Herek, a psychologist at the University of California at Davis, published a study in 1990 refuting the belief that homosexuals should not be teachers because they might sexually assault children. Instead, the doctor found, studies show overwhelmingly that child molesters are for the most part heterosexuals who are fixated on children. Despite the findings, many people believe flat out that gay equals child molester.

"Once parents perceive a threat to their children, their emotionality makes them prone to simplistic thinking," says Herek. "It is such emotionality that makes anti-gay stereotypes so hard to change." Many people also act out of adherence to religious orthodoxy in faiths that maintain homosexuality is a sin, the doctor said. "Their self-righteousness makes them feel they are acting morally when they attack homosexuals. It overcomes the normal inhibitions against aggression." And aggression is a problem — the U.S. National Gay and Lesbian Task Force shows a steadily increasing number of violent attacks against homosexuals during the 1980s and 90s.

Not all religious adherents follow the lead of the Catholic church. John Shelby Spong, an Episcopalian bishop in the U.S., says the Catholic stance is "antiquated," similar to its largely ignored ban on artificial birth control. Spong says the issue of homosexuality strikes at the very guts of the faith, dividing Christians into those who interpret the Bible literally, and those who view it metaphorically.

Says the bishop: "The only people who hold to the view that it's appropriate to discriminate against gays are Biblical fundamentalists — and, I fear, the Roman Catholic hierarchy — who quote passages out of the Bible to justify their prejudices. If you want to be literal, Leviticus 20 says that all homosexual people would be executed. I don't see anybody who's still quoting the Bible literally who still wants to go that far — not even Jerry Falwell."

Nevertheless, the silence around homosexuality takes a particularly violent toll in one segment of the population — teenagers. The U.S. Department of Health estimates that lesbian and gay youths are two to six times more likely to attempt suicide than other youths. The reason is not their sexual orientation, but rather the profound isolation and loneliness of growing up in a society which expects everyone to be heterosexual, a department report said.

"Lesbian and gay youth grow up with several strikes against them before they even discover or name their sexual orientation," the report noted. "At a young age, children observe society's dislike and disapproval of 'homosexuals.' As children enter adolescence, some discover (often to their great dismay) that they do not line up with society's expectations — they are not exclusively heterosexual. By this time, they have usually learned their lesson well — to dislike and disapprove of anything homosexual — and therein lies the seeds for spiralling self-hatred."

Gay children? To a dyed-in-the-wool heterosexual like me, the notion seemed difficult to accept. How can a little kid choose a gay lifestyle? And there it was again: the buzz phrase "gay lifestyle" — whereas the experts on such matters say it's not a choice at all, merely a fact of nature and hence, natural. While I as a child was thinking impure thoughts about the lovely Dale Evans, my sister was entertaining similar fantasies about teacher nuns. In adolescence and beyond, my fantasies would be accepted as appropriate while Lorraine's would be discouraged, hidden, secret. Brother and sister would spend half of their lives not sharing a fundamental fact about one of them until she ventured out of the closet.

In the classic study *Sexual Behavior and the Human*

Male, Alfred Kinsey wrote: "To those who believe, as children do, that conformance should be universal, any departure from the rule becomes immorality. The immorality seems particularly gross to an individual who is unaware of the frequency with which exceptions to the supposed rule actually occur."

How many Lorraines are there out there? Kinsey, the ground-breaking sex researcher, estimated that about 10 per cent of the populace is strictly homosexual, while the vast majority of individuals feel some homosexual urges or tendencies at some point in their lives. Other more recent and stringent surveys put the number of strict homosexuals at maybe 6 per cent, maybe 4. In July 1992, Statistics Canada released a fat package of information on Canadian families based on information collected from its most recent national census. Included were figures on how many Canadians are married, how many have children at home, and how many children they have. There was no mention of written-in information by homosexuals who told StatsCan about their living status. Tom Warner, spokesman for the Coalition for Lesbian and Gay Rights in Ontario, noted: "We're probably the only significant minority community for which data is not being collected. Frankly, it's offensive that we be excluded."

Whatever the numbers, it's just a numbers game. Once you get past the game, what remains is the reality: there are people out there who are different from me, and maybe from you. They're not just the front-line shock troops that you see at gay-pride parades — men mincing about in drag or woman shearing their heads and tattooing their bodies. They are our brothers, our sisters, our kids, our cousins, our co-workers, our neighbors, ourselves. Our families. My sister. That's the fact. All that's left to do is for us to accept the fact, and move on from there.

*A*nd the fact here was that my sister, in her early forties, married more than twenty years and with three children, had lived a lie most of her life. When I asked her, in preparation for this book, why she chose to tell me, an adoptive brother to whom she was not particularly close, Lorraine recalled: "I wanted my family to know. I knew it would be safe to tell you. At least you wouldn't be judgmental. After you found your mom, you changed, became more approachable, more open."

I hadn't noticed any discernible change in myself, but Lorraine had, and that was good enough for me. Trapped in her tiny community, Lorraine lacked the resources that my city provided. In the Yellow Pages I found the Vancouver Gay and Lesbian Centre, and Mary Brookes, a counselor there, gave me the names of other counselors who worked with older women just now venturing out of the closet. One of the women offered to meet Lorraine the next week. She was recently divorced, had three children, her husband was still supportive of her, accepting her sexual orientation.

I took Lorraine to the centre for her meeting with the counselor, and stood outside smoking cigarettes while I waited. An hour later Lorraine walked out. She couldn't stop the smile that spread across her face.

"Ricky, she's just like me!" she said. "She told me her story, and it was like listening to my story. Remember when I said I was all alone, that there was no one else like me? Well, I guess I was wrong."

Lorraine read more books and talked to more people, and eventually accepted that it was more unfair to Dave to stay with him than to leave. Lorraine thought it would be fairer to allow her daughters to stay at the family home, and she found a rental unit a few blocks away. It was the first time in her life she had lived alone.

It was the loneliest time of her life. There were times when she wished that Dave was nasty or ill-spirited or mean about being rejected. That way it would have been easier to put behind "the man who has been my life all of my life." Instead, he continues being supportive; the two act as co-parents, they told their daughters together about their mother's sexual orientation, and although the literature says there is no surefire way of knowing that a person — child or parent — will be able to accept homosexuality, none of the daughters has expressed any ill will toward their mom.

The Ouston family got together to celebrate mother Ann's 75th birthday, a barbecue at Sharon's back yard, one of the few times we've been together in the last decade or so that hasn't resulted from a funeral or other tragedy. A few days earlier, knowing that she'd be seeing her mother and tired of pretending everything was fine, Lorraine had written her a letter about her homosexuality, about the break-up of her family. There was no way of knowing how Ann might respond. The subject of gays had never come up in our house; Ann still attended church each Sunday; the literature on coming out stressed that many parents just won't accept reality and shun their children forever.

The first chance Ann had on the day of the barbecue, she slipped Lorraine an envelope. In the bathroom, Lorraine read the letter, written in the careful, cursive script that we remembered from the notes that Ann wrote us for school teachers.

"Dear Lorraine," the letter began, "I know how hard it

must have been for you to write this. I love you. You are my daughter."

Lorraine cried as her adoptive mother's letter went on to say how Ann would always consider Lorraine as her daughter, and if she ever brought anyone into her life, well, she would be family too. Dave, of course, would always be Ann's son-in-law, and welcome in her family, but Lorraine had to follow her heart. "This is one thing," Ann said, "that I don't agree with the church about. I hope one day they become more liberal in their thinking." The letter got passed around, from sister to brother, to cousin to friend, behind the backs of a cousin who had become a priest, and his mother who deemed gays as sinful. Ann Ouston, in the twilight of a lifetime, showed us a side we had never seen. We wept.

Times have not been all rosy. The woman that Lorraine met in her small town was transferred to a different city, the relationship deteriorated and finally collapsed. For the first time since her teens, she was left without a mate. And the clash with the Roman Catholic church "has left a big void in my life," she said. She searches still for something to fill the spiritual vacuum. "And sometimes I wish that we could have an evening of talking without the L word ever coming up."

As for the issue of adoption, her reluctance to go parent-hunting doesn't seem so odd now. The deepest questions Lorraine had unanswered were within her, and she needed to go exploring inside instead of searching outward. Every time we see each other she seems a little more satisfied and complete. Truth, and the acceptance of truth, will do that, I guess. Meanwhile, her circle of friends, straight and gay, grows ever wider, and her brother treasures the trust that his sister gave. These last two years we've felt the bond that siblings are supposed to have, and we value each other's company. We were adopted, a relationship that was thrust on us. Since then, we have adopted each other. There shall be no more secrets between us. It is the first time I've felt unconditional love for someone. It is a good feeling.

Six

In the business of journalism, sometimes it's just plain dumb luck that the story drops in your lap. Overhearing a chance remark, finding a secret document misfiled in a public file where it should not be, being at the right phone when a source decides to call a newsroom and tell all to whoever answers. Being in the right place at the right time. And, just as importantly, using your journalistic skills to listen, and pay attention.

That's how I found my brother.

It began as an easy way to make a hundred bucks. The CBC Radio department in Vancouver was holding a training course, bringing in hotshot producers to hone the skills of staffers working on radio news and current events shows. They would conduct mock interviews, then study what went right and what went wrong.

If there are tricks to conducting a successful interview, the most important one is similar to being at the right place at the right time. It's listening to whatever people say, and asking the proper follow-up question, getting your interviewees to elaborate on something they may have said that sounds like it might lead to somewhere interesting.

Poor interviewers follow a script: Question A, Question B, Question C, and so on. Good interviewers ask Question A, have a passel of questions in the bag ready to be dipped into as needed, but are also ready to chuck their questions out the window and take a different course if their subject says something unexpected.

It's like the reporter sent out to cover a meeting at city hall who comes back to the newsroom saying, "Sorry, there's no story. The meeting was canceled." Asked by his editor why the cancellation, the reporter replies, "Well, there was a fire, and city hall burned down, so the meeting's been scheduled for next week." While firing the reporter, the editor suggests that he might have thought of filing a story on the destruction of city hall.

No brain surgery, just developing a nose for news.

For the training program to work, the radio trainers needed real live subjects to interview. The executive producer for radio, Liz Hughes, was asked to think of a couple of interesting people who would play along with wannabe interviewers. Liz had worked with noted Canadian actress Janet Wright on a radio pilot project, and was taken with Wright's informality, sense of fun and ability to tell a story. So Wright became the "celebrity" interviewee, and Liz suggested that I might be worthwhile to interview on several other topics — adoption, stuttering, investigative journalism, whatever. There would be a nominal fee, $100, for the day. I love talking about myself, and anytime someone offers me money to do it, I figure it's a bonus. Janet Wright and I arrived at the CBC studios in Vancouver, steeled for a full day of being interviewed by people who don't necessarily know how to interview.

Most of the junior journalists chose to talk about adoption. So I told the story of Mo, responding to questions that were sometimes on topic and sometimes not. Some interviewers elicited interesting insights and anecdotes, sometimes the interviewers got bogged down trying to pursue avenues that just weren't there. So the story got told again and again.

Heading the training course, and sitting in the back of the room listening to my repetitions, was a Toronto producer called Dave Candow. After the fourth or fifth time he heard me mention Corner Brook, Candow spoke up.

"I was born there too," he said, offering a couple of reminiscences of his boyhood home. Dave Candow is a senior journalist. He looked to be about 55 or so. About the age my father would have been, if he had lived. They were from the same town. It was a small town.

After lunch, in the hallway outside the subterranean studios, I put the question to him: "Did you know a man called Donald O'Connor?"

"Oh yes," said Dave Candow. In fact, he said, Donald's widow married Dave's brother.

"Donald's widow? He got married then?"

"Oh yes," said Dave Candow. "Not long before he died." In fact, he said, the Candow family helped raise young Michael.

"Young Michael?"

"Don's son," said Dave Candow.

Donald had a son with his wife, and he died when his son was just a young boy. The son's name was Michael. He lived with his grandparents now, back in the Newfoundland town where his father was born. His grandparents. My grandparents.

My grandparents were alive, then. Both of them, the mother and father of my father.

When Mo had said that Donald was dead, I felt that part of my heritage was dead as well. There was no one else who knew about me, probably. Forcing myself onto unknown distant relatives could expose Mo's secret, and anyway, what was the point? It was my father's genes that I carried, and my father was dead.

But I hadn't thought that my father may have passed those genes on to another. He had, and his name was Michael.

"Oh yes," said Dave Candow. "And Michael works for the CBC, in Newfoundland, in television."

Just like me. It's in the genes, I thought.

There wasn't much that Dave Candow could say about young Don. "He was a bit of a bon vivant," he said, smiling half a smile. A way with the ladies.

Dave had not known that Don had gotten at least one of the ladies in quite a way — the family way, as they used to say.

Don was a hockey player, and coach, like his father before him. He sold Electrolux vacuum cleaners to pay his way. And he was a Protestant. Back in the fifties, said Candow, the Prods and Papists despised each other as much as they do back in Northern Ireland today. The shame of Mo being pregnant and unmarried would have been less than the shame her parents would feel knowing their Catholic daughter was consorting with a Protestant, said the son of Newfoundland.

As he spoke, remembering the old days, Dave's accent grew thicker, the Newfoundland drawl that's faintly reminiscent of lilting Irish speech.

I stood in the hallway, talking to Dave, talking to the only person I'd known other than my mother who had known my father. And he also knew my brother, my half-brother, the half that shared my genes.

In the news business, you learn to adapt quickly to new information. Assassinations, wars breaking out, peace breaking out, tragic accidents. Grab the new piece of information, no matter how calamitous, digest it and do a story, quickly, on deadline. Today's new information concerned a whole other human being I hadn't thought existed. Standing in the hall, talking with Dave Candow, I was happy not to have to report a story about this new brother. In truth, I didn't know what to think.

That night, at home, I wrote a letter to Michael O'Connor.

The letter had to be vague about Mo. I couldn't risk exposing her secrets. And it had to be as neutral as possible, nothing overwhelmingly sentimental to a young man who may not give a lot of credence to sentimentality.

After telling Michael my name, and the fact that I worked for the CBC (Hey brother! We've got something in common!), out it came.

> I was adopted at birth, and recently tracked down my roots, and my birth parents. Michael, this may come as something of a shock, but I've just learned that your father was also my father.
>
> Donald O'Connor, who died in a car crash in 1968.
>
> He dated a local girl back in 1955. She got pregnant, didn't tell her family, crossed the country to hide her pregnancy, gave birth to me, then went away. She and Donald had talked about getting married; it didn't work out. She eventually moved down to the States, where I found her happily married, with four kids.
>
> She told me the name of my father, your father. I combed through Corner Brook records, learned he had died, and thought: "Well, that's that." Donald's parents — your grandparents — didn't know about the pregnancy, and they probably wouldn't have approved of the woman who was my mother. She was Catholic, your father was Protestant, back then the two didn't mix.

"So, I didn't know about you. But last week I met a family friend of yours by the name of Dave Candow," the letter said, going on at some length to outline the innocent way I stumbled onto Michael's existence.

> *After 36 years of not knowing, it's kind of strange learning you have a half-brother living in the other end of the country. And I imagine it's peculiar for you to read this now.*
>
> *Michael, I don't know what I hope to achieve by writing this letter. I do know the letter comes with no strings attached. Dave told me you didn't have any brothers or sisters, so I thought you might want to know you have a half-brother living over here.*

There. Nothing mushy. Keep it straightforward. Don't pressure the lad.

> *Dave told me your father was tall, athletic and a good looking guy, so I guess most of my genes came from my mother's side. But it was interesting to learn that you work for the Mother Corp. There must be some genetic connection there.*

Some brief biographical material, then, the easy out. I don't want Michael to get freaked out and throw the letter away. As a young guy he's probably not going to respond immediately, so I'll give him some breathing room.

> *I don't know how you're going to react to this. You might choose to ignore it and throw it away, and that's your right. You might choose to mull it over for a while, and that's your right, too. You might choose to write me or phone, I don't know. And if you contact*

me, you might tell me not to bug you any more. Un-
derstand, Michael, as a reporter I've been told to bugger
off by the best, so if that's your reaction, I'd understand.

Frankly, I don't know what my first reactions would
be if I got news like this.

And I don't know if you'll choose to tell your grand-
parents about me. They might be pleased to know. They
might be angered or upset. I don't know them; you do.
I suspect it might be wiser to leave them in the dark
for now. I also have to be careful to continue protecting
the identity of my birth mother. She still has family in
Corner Brook, I'm still the "secret" from her past, and
it's not my right to reveal her secret.

So there you have it. I'll leave it with you. Maybe
one day we can have a beer together.

Sincerely,
Rick Ouston.

The library provided a phone book with Michael's address, I mailed the letter and waited for a reply.

It never came.

*M*ore than a year had gone by between finding my
mother and meeting her. During that time we
spoke on the phone maybe a dozen times. Each time, she
had to place the call, at night, her husband asleep, she
feigning insomnia, waiting two time zones away to place
a collect call to her son so the phone bill would not betray
her secret.

"I love you," she would say. "You know what? I love
you." Emphasis on the word love, drawing it out, loooov-
vve, perhaps to prove to her son that she did, perhaps

just to emphasize the point in case her son was too dim to realize that she did. Does. Separated by lifetimes and national boundaries, the late-night telephone was the only way my mother could tell the son she bore what mothers have told their children throughout time. Over the long-distance line we talked small talk of little consequence, jobs for me, the doings of her children for her.

Talking on the phone, my mother quickly learned that her son has a speech impediment, a stutter. There had been no money for speech therapists in the Ouston family budget, and Ann and Fred thought their son would grown out of his "nervous condition." Doctors have since determined that stuttering is more than likely a physiological problem, some kind of screw-up between the brain and the hundred or so muscles it takes to make speech. Us stutterers can develop tricks to make us sound almost fluent, but in reality people like me stutter hundreds and thousands of times a day. Researchers feel stuttering is likely genetic, occurring in families. No one else in the extended Ouston family stuttered. But Mo recalled that she had a brother who stuttered.

"We'd say the Lord's Prayer, and my father would make him stop every time he stuttered and say it again," she said. For her, just something that happened in her family. For me, it was the first time in my life I could point to an ancestor and say: "Hey! I'm just like him!" Not quite having Uncle So-and-so's skill in music or mom's athletic prowess, but it was something. By the slip of my tongue, I now felt context, a belonging to the family of man.

For her son, the phone calls were the only reinforcement of the fact that he had found his mother. Between calls, during the weeks and months in which there was no word from Mo, there was always the possibility that the last phone call had been the last. People die. They get sick, and die, sometimes slowly. Perhaps Mo was lying in a hospital bed somewhere, her life ebbing, fading, unable to make another secret call to her son, afraid to ask a nurse for help. Maybe she'd been hit by a bus, killed in a car accident, just another statistic, a one-inch story in a regional newspaper somewhere. I would never know of Mo's death. No one would know to tell me she had died.

So each call from Mo was precious; each call said she was alive. A reaffirmation of reunion, coupled with the banishment of morbid thoughts. When the phone rang and the voice on the line said, "This is the AT&T operator. Will you accept a collect call from Mo?" what I heard was: My mother is alive.

And each time, ringing off, the possibility that the next time we speak, we will speak in person. During the months, I became pushier, more persistent, for a personal meeting, until she finally relented and it was done.

I treasured the phone calls.

I hated the phone calls.

When the operator asked if I would accept a collect call from Mo, I was again cast into the role of the son my mother cannot have. During the time leading up to the meeting, there was for me at least the possibility of getting something out of the calls: a touch, a glance, a meeting that would provide memories good enough for a lifetime. Now that we had met, the phone calls seemed only to reinforce the separation and to magnify the deception. Mo wanted to tell her son she loves him, something that every mother should have the right and ability to say. She could only do that on the phone. That the love she espoused was not reciprocated by her son wasn't really her problem. And if she could say the words, then quickly hang up, it wouldn't have become much of a problem for her son. But the trap lay in the words between "I love you" and "Goodbye." The small talk about the lives of her sons and daughter and in-laws and grandchildren rankled. It was all she knew, and it was good enough to provide conversation material for millions of mothers like her, but to me it sounded like babble about people I don't know, will never know, must never know, and it was a reminder that although I am her son, I cannot be her son. Our relationship is tethered by mere telephone cable, and although I know that Mo is trying to be all the mother she can be, the telephone relationship seems somehow mocking. I have no way to know when she may phone, and each time she does it is an unbidden reminder that no matter what we want, we can't have it.

I come to dread the calls. And they come more frequently after our meeting. In the American west, a woman waits for her husband's snores so she can tell her son she loves him. She has held her son, has met him and trusts him, knows that he can tie a tie and afford airplane tickets and has made a life for himself. She wants her son to know his mother loves him.

In Vancouver, at night, the city asleep and quiet, the only sound jazz from the stereo, a nightcap in hand, idly stroking Lou the cat and winding down from another day, her son hopes the telephone does not ring. And when it does, he hopes not to hear the sound of the AT&T operator.

It goes on for months, the late-night calls going nowhere. By not telling my mother what I really feel, I am lying to her. By telling her not to call, at least not so often, I risk losing her. No matter how it's phrased, Mo will likely interpret the words to mean an end. That her son wants her out of his life. I don't want to hurt my mother. I don't want to hurt myself.

I take the risk.

Friday. Midnight. The telephone rings. It is Mo. "I love you," she says. During the past month she has called five times, maybe six.

We chat, the usual routine, and I take a deep breath and say: "Mo, Mom, I don't want you to take this the wrong way, but you've been calling a lot, and I really wish that you wouldn't, you know, so often? I mean, I want to hear from you, I want to know you're okay, that everything's going all right, but we really don't have much to talk about. And I really don't want to be the son you can't have. You feel sorry every time we speak, and I feel sad, and, well, I just don't want to keep on feeling that way. Do you understand what I'm saying?"

"Yes." The voice is dull. Flat. "I love you. Goodbye, my darling." She hangs up.

I wonder when my mother will call next. For more than a year, I keep on wondering.

Seven

*O*ne down, one to go.

My mother's name is no longer a secret to her son. That means a way around the damnable chicken-and-egg dilemma surrounding her first born. The Nova Scotia government had refused to release any information about my sister until I could provide them the name of our mother. They demanded that the wall of secrets around the identity of our mother be breached before they revealed anything, even non-identifying information, about my sister. Now that wall has fallen. Now her son knows her name, even the place where she gave birth to my sister. My mother refers to her daughter as an "incident." Her brother thinks of her as a sister.

She hasn't registered with the government agency in Nova Scotia. If she registered, the government worker bees would be able to match her request to mine. But if she doesn't know she's adopted, she wouldn't register. And if she doesn't know she's adopted, does anyone have the right to impose the truth on her? "Oh by the way, ma'am, just thought you'd like to know, you know your family, your mom and dad? Well, they're not."

If the people who had adopted my sister kept the truth from her, would anyone be served by exposing her life as a lie? Well, I would be served, my curiosity satiated. But would her life be improved knowing the truth? Or could it cause great grief and anguish? These were the questions that had troubled me about looking for my sister since learning about her fifteen years earlier. Now she was fifteen years older, and the troubling questions hadn't gone away. They were tempered, however, by the new knowledge that our mother hadn't registered with any registry either, but had been glad to be found. Maybe my sister would feel that way.

Maybe my sister would resent the intrusion into her life. I might find her dead, and that would end the search. Or I might find her, then use whatever journalistic abilities I have to winkle out whether she knows about her adoption.

Or I could track down her adoptive parents and ask them if their daughter knew she wasn't their daughter. That was one way around the dilemma. Don't hunt for the girl. Hunt for the folks. If her parents are found, and they have kept the adoption a secret, offer them the chance to set the record straight. They would have two options: tell her, or tell me to go away. If they refused to come clean, I would go away. It would be unconscionable to intrude so late in a life.

Until now, the only leads I had were that my sister was born in Nova Scotia in 1954, and that she may have been given the same last name as my mother gave me. Since she had likely been adopted, that name would have changed shortly after birth. Since she was female, it is likely her last name has changed since then through marriage. Since she shares my genes, it is possible her last name has changed again through divorce and remarriage.

So far my sister was little more than an anonymous (to me) female born in Nova Scotia but living now God knows where. Or, perhaps, no longer living. A victim of crib death, maybe, or a car accident in her twenties. Maybe she's alive but doesn't know she's adopted. Looking for an unknown person in an unknown place widens the parameters of the search considerably. But now the search pattern would be narrowed. Now I know the name of her mother. Our mother.

Once again, I write a letter to Nova Scotia, this time containing the secret of our mother's name, and identifying the town of Sydney where the first secret was left.

And by return mail from Nova Scotia comes a letter, marked Private and Confidential.

"Dear Mr. Ouston," it says. "We have a record of your previous correspondence and our difficulty in positive identification of your sister's adoption records. With the information you have now provided we were able to locate the file and we are able to share with you the non-identifying information on her adoptive family. We are not able to provide you with identifying material or do a search for her."

Your sister was born July 2, 1954, in Sydney, Nova Scotia and was placed with her adoptive family in October, 1954. The couple were residents of Nova Scotia. They were of French descent and Roman Catholic. They had been married for twelve years and had one son, age eight.

The adopting father was in his early 30's. Both his parents were deceased but he had two brothers. He had completed grade 12 and went on to complete a trade course. He was employed in a managerial position in a private business and earned a comfortable income. He was 5'7" tall with dark hair and coloring. He was a friendly, pleasant person.

The adopting mother was in her early 30's, at the time of the adoption. She grew up in a stable family with four brothers. She had completed Grade 10 and had worked in a clerk position until her marriage. She did not work outside the home at the time of the adoption. She was an attractive woman, about 5'3" tall with red hair.

The family owned their own home in an urban area. It was a comfortable, three bedroom house which they had remodeled. It was nicely furnished with excellent housekeeping standards. The neighborhood was very suitable for children with schools and other services nearby.

They were a couple who seemed to get along well together and were successfully parenting their eight year old son. They placed a high value on education and it was thought they would encourage a child in this area.

The couple were overjoyed to learn that Rosalind had been chosen for them and she made an excellent adjustment to her new home. The social worker's last visit to the home was in October, 1955. In her report she noted that Rosalind was a pretty child with dark eyes and brown hair. She started walking at eleven months and was developing quite a vocabulary. The family was delighted with her and she was receiving excellent care and much love.

After the normal period of time had passed the adoption was granted and we have no further record of contact with her or her adoptive parents. Your name is on the Adoption Reunion Register and if your sister should contact us, we will certainly let you know. Although I know you are anxious to notify her, we will

have to wait until she contacts us. Please remember to
keep us advised of any address changes.
I hope this information is helpful to you.

It was not.

Essentially, all that the two-page letter said was that a
generic baby was adopted by Nova Scotia Ward and June
Cleaver clones. My sister as The Beaver in a happy family
tableau. The letter did contain a name — Rosalind — but
that was likely her original name, the name that her mother
bestowed on the dark-eyed pretty baby before leaving her.
The file from which the letter was derived would have
contained much more — the names of the parents, their
address and phone numbers, the place where the father
worked, schools and names of relatives. Those bits of information would have made finding this unknown woman
a cinch. But that information was deemed an official secret
by the provincial legislators who make the laws governing
adoption in their province. Ultimately, that law told her
brother to go suck eggs.

And she still hadn't registered with the reunion registry
in Nova Scotia. That could mean many things:

- She wasn't interested in finding her biological par-
  ents and didn't want to be found;
- She didn't know she was adopted;
- She didn't know about the registry;
- She didn't know the province of her birth;
- She was dead; or
- A combination of the above.

The only fact in the letter that was new was that
Rosalind had been adopted by a Roman Catholic couple.
That made sense. The church handled the babies of bad
Catholic girls before the state stepped in. Bad Catholic

girls gave birth to babies and Catholics took the babies away and gave them to other Catholics. It was obvious that whoever had adopted my sister would have been members of the church. Anyone else would have been deemed unworthy of owning a genuine Catholic baby.

My first attempt at following a paper trail began and ended with the Catholic church. Records indicated that I had been baptized a month after my birth, before being adopted. The original records called me Paul Anthony Griffin. The records had been altered back in 1957 to make it appear that the baby was legitimately who he is today, and not some bastard spawn. That meant that either Mo, or the church-sponsored orphanage, had arranged for my baptism as quickly as possible.

There is a reason for the separation of church and state: both keep their own sets of records.

The letter about my sister gave a birthdate of July 2, 1954. If the routine around me was followed with Mo's first child, it would have meant that a baby named Rosalind Griffin was baptized in Sydney, Nova Scotia, in the weeks following July 2, 1954. That would narrow down the hunt for any Catholic clerk who was asked to dig up an old baptismal certificate out of church files. And that certificate would have been updated and altered to reflect the new reality bestowed by the state — including the new adopted name, and the names of adoptive parents.

Church records are available to any member of the public, depending on just how helpful or persnickety the guardian of those files happens to be. That means that you can walk in off the street and ask politely to see record books. You'll have a lot more success and raise fewer suspicions if you never use the A word — adoption — and instead couch your quest in terms of "family trees" and genealogical history. Requests for information by mail are responded to in as timely a fashion as possible. If you really want to make a good impression, have a ranking member of the particular church in question make the request for you. It can be a local parish priest or preacher, perhaps a nun who taught you, or a sympathetic lay person with standing in the denomination in question.

As it happens, I knew a Catholic priest and asked him to write his counterpart in Sydney, Nova Scotia, for a baptism record for a baby girl, born July 2, 1954, likely christened Rosalind Griffin.

A couple of weeks later my contact phoned me.

"Rick, do you have a pen? Good. Here it is. Her name is Cherisse Eileen Thibeault." He spells it out. "Her parents are Stanley and Eilleen. Two Ls for Eilleen. You didn't get it from me."

And there it was.

Cherisse. My sister's name is Cherisse. Nice name. I wonder how she'll feel when she learns she has a brother?

First stop, the telephone. Let your fingers do the walking. The long-distance directory assistance operator in Nova Scotia has no listing in Sydney for a Cherisse Thibeault, or for a Stanley, or an Eilleen with two Ls.

In downtown Vancouver, then, to the main branch of the public library, where they keep every telephone book published in Canada. (Most libraries now have the contents of telephone books freely available on CD-ROM computer databases; you can cover the continent in minutes.) The stack of phone books for Nova Scotia lists no Cherisse or Stanley or Eilleen. Phone books for other nearby provinces don't either.

They could be dead. They could be unlisted. They could have moved, to another province, another country. Maybe they joined the southward migration to the U.S., or travelled across the Atlantic to England. They could be any-where. Abducted by UFOs, for all I know.

In Vancouver, the Church of Jesus Christ of Latter-Day Saints maintains a branch of the Mormon Family History Centre. The main church in Salt Lake City is famous for its compilations of family trees and historical backgrounds from around the world. Less well known is the fact that church branches run their own centres, replete with micro-fiched copies of the master originals in Salt Lake. A day in the centre, scanning records on microfilm reading ma-chines, told me there were many Thibeaults in many places in the world, but no records for Stanleys married to Eilleens begetting Cherisses. No mention of a Cherisse, either. For alternative spellings, the microfiche documents said, try Tibo, Tybo, Teebo, Thebeault, Thibault, Theobold, Thebault ... the list went on.

From the library telephone books for Nova Scotia, I had recorded the names and addresses of the thirty or so people named Thibeault.

"Dear Thibeault family," the letter I wrote began. "I am trying to locate members of a family named Thibeault who lived in Nova Scotia in 1954." It went on to give the names of Stanley and Eilleen, the vague physical descrip-tions from the Nova Scotia government, and the name of Cherisse. The information I knew, and the information I didn't know.

"It's not much to go on, I know, but it is a matter of urgent family concern," the letter said, never mentioning the word adoption. "Because the mails are slow, if you have any information which might help, please phone me, collect."

The letters were mailed September 17, 1989.

No one ever called.

You learn two things as a reporter. One, to constantly be on the lookout for news, for stories, to see what's available, what tidbit might lend itself to development into a story. The old movies called it "having a nose for news." In reality, it's all just part of the daily hustle to fill the limitless maw of empty pages, daily deadlines, something to put in the newscast to separate the ads. Just as important, selfish as it sounds, is the need to produce stories so that publishers and editors are satisfied that your paycheque is earned. It's a mindset that forces journalists to keep a tiny portion of their walnut-sized brains open to a chance comment, perhaps overheard, that may lead to a story. It's not that we're constantly straining to steal people's private communications and turn them into News McNuggets ... it's just that, well, once you turn on the information-gathering antennae, they stay on, and it's hard to turn them off.

And that leads to the second thing: keeping one's ears open. The newsrooms of most local newspaper and TV newsrooms contain scanning devices which monitor radio communications among police officers and firefighters. The machines bark a constant cacophony of electronic drivel which newsies learn to block out like any other background noise, training themselves to listen only for important messages like "Man with a gun!" or "Shots fired" — communications which might develop into a violent crime worthy of news coverage. The rest of the communications go heard but unheeded, a blah-blah-blah of white noise, but pens stop and phones go on hold when the magical violent crime announcements blast cryptically over the monitors.

Some of my best stories have come from chance comments overheard. Like the time I found myself on a flight to Ottawa, sitting beside a public art gallery employee, enjoying the free drinks. (Such business-class flyers are often referred to as Pigs in Space.) Canvasses worth hundreds of thousands of dollars had recently been stolen from Canada's National Gallery, and gallery officials weren't talking. But this employee was giggling about how the national news media were speculating about a high-tech thief, while staffers knew that security was so lax at the gallery that the heist had been pulled off by a visitor who had merely slit the canvasses from a bound volume and walked away. There were no alarms, no baggage checks. It had been little more than a high-value shoplifting job. I ordered us more drinks, heard the tale, and had a front-page national story the moment I stepped off the plane.

Luck, pure and simple, and taking advantage of that luck. And being pushy enough to turn the luck into a tangible benefit.

So it was at a summer barbecue in the back yard of CBC Radio executive Liz Hughes in North Vancouver. Idle chit-chat of the "what's new" variety between a gaggle of guests had prompted radio producer Cathy Simons to note that her significant other, Joe Moulins, was spending the summer at a radio job in Sydney, Nova Scotia.

I was standing nearby, talking with Liz's husband Doug Rushton, cocktail chatter in the background sounding like blah-blah-blah-blah SYDNEY! MAN WITH A GUN! SHOTS FIRED! Sydney: Birthplace of the elusive Cherisse Eileen Thibeault, née Rosalind Griffin. Last known address of this unknown person who is my sister. Also known as "the other time," or "the other incident," by Mo the mom. Sydney, where the trail grew cold. Nova Scotia, where all the

Thibeaults in all the province didn't know or didn't respond to my requests for information about Stanley and Eilleen.

Eavesdropping in earnest now, I listened as Cathy talked about joining Joe for a vacation that August.

I had appeared on Cathy's *Almanac* lunchtime radio program to talk about adoption issues, so she knew my story and about my search. And I knew, from the times I had visited fellow newsies in towns I didn't know, how it would be for Cathy in Sydney. For the first few days she'd visit the local newsrooms (and they all look the same) and trade lies and current gossip with the local members of her guild, spend a few more days seeing the sights of the new city, then ... get bored. I knew that Cathy would end up with time on her hands while Joe worked at the radio station. And yes, she would be on vacation, trying to relax after months of cranking out daily radio programs, but it was worth a shot.

"Look, this is kind of an imposition," I said, "but if you're gonna be in Sydney, there is a favor I'd like to ask, if it's possible."

We talked about adoption, and my searches, and my being too cheap or too lazy or too whatever it was that was preventing me from completing the hunt for this unknown sister. I explained about the letters going unanswered, about not wanting to blanket Nova Scotia with expensive long-distance phone calls, and suggested that if the name turned up easily anywhere, it would be appreciated. A couple of days later I faxed a short note with the skimpy facts I knew about Rosalind/Cherisse, her parents and birthdate, with an apology for inflicting myself on their holidays, and left it at that.

Of course there was no guarantee anything would come of my heavy-handed request to impose on their vacation. Young lovers separated by a continent and by months may deem other things more important than seeking a stranger as a favor for someone who was little more than a stranger himself.

However, in Nova Scotia, unknown to me, the journalistic instincts of Cathy Simons and Joe Moulins had overwhelmed whatever other instincts might have been in play. The only Thibeault in the Sydney phone book had never heard of Stanley or Eileen or Cherisse and could offer nothing. One phone call, a trail dead. There were no other Thibeaults to call. Then Cathy, or Joe, had one of those little flashes of brilliance which separate ordinary journalists from the higher order. While there was just one lone Thibeault in the telephone directory, Cathy and Joe noticed a great whacking swathe of surnames spelled T-H-E-B-E-A-U-L-T. Not content to drop the hunt with a single call, they took a shot despite the spelling disparity and called a randomly chosen Thebeault.

Stanley was dead, they were told by the first Thebeault they phoned, but his sister is still alive in Welland, Ontario. Within an hour Cathy had talked with Stanley's sister and had been given a location for Cherisse's brother in Ohio.

Thebeault. Her name was Thebeault, not Thibeault. An "e" instead of an "i." For two years the facts of my sister's life had been blocked from me because somewhere between the Catholic records office in Sydney and my own handwritten notes from a phone conversation, the surname had been misspelled. Maybe by a clerk updating a baptismal certificate years ago, maybe by the two priests as the information was passed cross country, maybe by my source as he relayed the information to me, maybe even by myself.

A bloody spelling error, for heaven's sake, had blocked the hunt for this unknown sister. Now the path was cleared. Elation, tempered with a dash of fear. Finding the truth, and the facts, isn't always pretty. As with my father, there was a chance I'd find my sister long dead. Or a pathetic junkie. Maybe she is alive, healthy and happy, and doesn't know about her adoption. Is it my right to interfere in her life, her past? If she doesn't know, do I tell her? If she isn't alive, do I have a solitary wake for a sister I've never known? If I do find her, will Lorraine and Sharon feel threatened, or sad, or jealous? Lorraine has just placed her trust in me. Do I jeopardize that trust now and risk losing a sister I already love? Crush out a cigarette, light another, the trail is warm, littered with questions.

Reid is the name of her brother in Ohio, Cathy had reported. Brother? I am her brother. My birth, my life, my genes give me the right to know what her other brother knows. How can this man be the brother of my sister? Another, earlier adoption? Or a natural son, conceived by Stanley and Eilleen, a biological family later complemented by Cherisse's adoption? Will Reid feel threatened, or welcome this intrusion from the secret past? There are many reasons not to follow this path.

I make the call to Ohio.

Yes, he says, this is Reid Thebeault. And yes, his parents were Stanley and Eilleen. Both gone now. And yes, they adopted a baby girl they named Cherisse. And yes, he said, Cherisse knows about her adoption. And yes, "Cherisse is my sister."

BINGO!

Cherisse IS! Not "was." Is. Is alive. Not dead, like my father who I find and found him dead. My father. Our father who art no more. Is. Is, within reach. Is, going to get found by a brother she knows nothing about. Is. It is a good word, is. Short, simple, but fraught with meaning, and with promise.

And she knows of her adoption. That means my intrusion into her life would not make her earlier life a lie.

That means I can barge into whatever life she has today. Full steam ahead.

Where is she now?

Reid skips a beat and says, "I ... I don't know."

He pauses, saying "ummm, ummm," like a mantra to the god of ignorance. "I guess it doesn't sound good, losing track of my only sister, and me being her only brother. She sent me a Christmas card last year, but I can't find it. I know it was some little town in west Texas in the middle of nowhere, but I just can't remember where." Reid was older when Cherisse was adopted, the two were never close, he went away to school, the two never bonded.

On the telephone, in Vancouver, I find it hard to resist telling Reid what I think of a brother who would lose track of his only sister. I want to call him a lout. A twit. A flea. More vulgar terms come to mind. I must shove the words back down my throat. I must be polite with this man, or he will surely hang up the phone. Here, in Vancouver, I'm trying to uncover the identity of a sister I've never known, while this guy has chosen to lose track of the only sister he ever knew. It is hard to keep the iciness and sarcasm from my voice. If he hangs up now, the trail might grow cold again.

What can you tell me about her, I ask.

Reid knows this: she had married a man named Combs in Galveston, Texas. The husband was a firefighter, killed on the job some years earlier. Cherisse had two kids, she left Galveston, he couldn't remember when. End of story.

We hang up, Reid apologizing and promising to try to find out more, me fighting an ugly rage that must be left unspoken. Put the phone down, light a cigarette. Don't get angry. Stay calm. The missing link to all this turns out to be the kind of man who can manage to lose track of his only sibling ... Stop it. This kind of thinking doesn't help.

Combs. He said she married a man named Combs.

Probably took his name. Cherisse Combs. Long distance to Galveston directory assistance determines there is no Cherisse or C. Combs in the directory.

Keep it simple, stupid. What do I know? He worked for the fire department and was killed on the job. I don't know about Texas law, but there must have been some kind of pension, death benefits, workers' compensation, something for the spouse or the kids he left behind.

"Do you have a listing, operator, for the Galveston fire department? A non-emergency number?"

The switchboard shuffle finally winds up at the desk of a woman who says yes, she keeps track of payments to family members of firefighters killed on the job but no, she can't confirm or deny that we have a Cherisse Combs, or any children, as a beneficiary. It's policy, sir.

You can't ask a clerk to change policy. Policies are made by bureaucrats and politicians, not by people who answer their own phones. Policies are set on high, and it is the job of the workers to abide by those policies no matter how frustrating it may be.

Policy. Maybe based on an individual's right to privacy; maybe on the realization that the person seeking information might be a process server or a bill collector and that the clerk would be doing her client a disservice if she revealed her whereabouts.

But you learn, in searching for information, to remember the focus of the search: you are not seeking to change policies. You are looking for a person. If this powerless clerk on the telephone is hamstrung by the orders of her bureaucratic masters, then you must try to circumvent the policy. Tell the clerk you understand.

"Ma'am? I'm not asking you to confirm or deny anything. But I want you to understand that Cherisse is my sister. She was adopted at birth. So was I. We're brother and sister, and she doesn't know anything about me. All I'm asking is this: don't tell me whether or not you know Cherisse, or where she is. Just do this: phone her. Tell her I'm trying to find her. Take down my name and phone number and phone her. Don't tell me if you're going to do it or not. Just do it. Please."

I give the woman my name and number, and wait.

*M*y sister's current name and her whereabouts are still a mystery. The thread runs from Newfoundland to Colorado to Nova Scotia to Ohio to Texas and now ... she is lost again. Her name had been Rosalind and Griffin, then Cherisse and Thibeault, then Thebeault, then Combs, and now ... likely remarried, with yet another surname.

An unknown stranger in a strange land might get a call from a pension clerk, and then again she might not. She might decide to return the call, she might not. It's easier to dismiss a request from a third party than to ignore a flesh-and-blood sibling on the line. Michael, my half-brother in Newfoundland, Donald O'Connor's son, is not responding to my letter. It has been months. Maybe Cherisse will choose to leave it for months as well. Maybe she's scared. Maybe she thinks I want something of her. Money, that's what they want in the movies. Maybe she fears I'm a junkie, or some pathetic jerk still whining about his infant adoption, never able to get on with his own life. Get a life, is maybe what she's saying; get on with it. Maybe she'll call me, and we'll just plain dislike each other. The southern states are stereotypes to me, chockablock full of born again Christians and Ku Klux Klansmen. She might accept me only if I accept Jesus Christ as my own personal savior. Maybe she sews white hoods into the night and proclaims herself Grand Dragonette of the Imperial Knights of the KKK. That would be unacceptable, and the trail would end there. The reunion would not last long. Reunion, again, is the wrong word. We never were united, so cannot be united again. And although the fact of her life has preyed on mine, the fact of mine is unknown to her. You don't miss what you don't know, they say. We don't know each other. Never have. Maybe never will. Maybe it's best that way.

The phone rings.

A man asks for me, and tells me his name. His speech is slurred. Words are forced, stretched to ridiculous proportion, slowed. If you've ever walked into a cocktail party very late, maybe stuck at work so you're stone cold sober while the other partiers are already into their cups, you know what it's like to listen to a voice numbed by alcohol through ears not yet brought down to the same speed. Boring, frustrating, embarrassing. Through numb lips he says something that sounds like: "Ah unnnerstann ya bin traaahn ta connact mah whaaafff."

Mah whaaaff. My wife. Possessive, as in: My dog. My house. My wife. Oh God, I hadn't thought of this. What happens if Cherisse is married to some white trash cracker who's gonna decide what his woman will and will not do? What happens if? What happens now?

The drunken man continues his stuporous rant. My stomach heaves. After all these years, after finding our mother, after finding our father, after finding each other, it's going to end here, a faceless drunk deciding that the facts of our lives will go unshared. The man continues talking, slurring. His wife has been through a lot of hardship and doesn't need to get hurt anymore. He asks me how I traced her, and how I knew the connection was real, and after a few moments of listening, the realization sets in ... this man is not drunk. This man is speaking with a thick Texas accent and drawl, like the ones I've heard in movies, only in movies the drawl is speeded up so the audience doesn't lose patience. In the same way people assume I'm stoned or brain-damaged because of my stutter, I have assumed the talking man is impaired by alcohol, and not by simple regional speech patterns.

The not-drunken man is named Robert Fowler. He talks of how he married Cherisse and her kids last year, of how they moved to Robert's home town of Andrews in West Texas to get away from the big-city problems of Galveston, and "if you want to speak to your sister, she's right here. Cherisse, it's your biological brother." The sound of a phone passing from one person to another.

Time for a snappy first line. I can't think of one. Instead, I say: "Hi there."

Real cool, Rick. That'll sure leave an impression. Hi there. The first words spoken by brother to sister. Not exactly the stuff of immortal first lines. Call me Ishmael. Now that's an opening line. It was the best of times, it was the worst of times. Legendary. In the beginning God created the heaven and the earth. And, hi there. I feel relief at her response: "Hi!" Good. She couldn't think of a snappy one either. Okay, we're even. She's also got a Texas accent, stretching out a simple "hi" into a multi-syllabic rendering worthy of cheesy Hee-Haw humor except this isn't Hee-Haw and she isn't drunk either and we've talked for the first time. I am talking with my sister.

Cherisse wants to know how I found her. I tell her the story of her birth registration, the baptism certificate, the Rosalind Griffin-Cherisse Thibeault connection and the misspelling, when she stops me and says: "Rosalind? My name was Rosalind?" I stop blurting out the facts of the hunt;

to her this must be sounding like a call from the KGB: "We know things about you that you don't know yourself." In the space of a few seconds Cherisse has learned her original name, the identity of her mother and father and her birthplace, and the fact that her mother's alive and her father is not, and the reason she's not saying anything isn't because she's bored ... it's because she's overloaded.

Slow down, Rick.

Cherisse says "Oh my God" a lot, punctuating each new fact with another homage to the supreme being. But the things she hasn't said are just as important. She hasn't said: "What do you want?" She hasn't said: "I don't want to know." She hasn't said: "Leave me alone." She's letting her brother do the talking for now because the brother knows things she wants to know, and, as it turns out, things she has wanted to know for a long time.

Cherisse Thebeault was eleven when she learned, through accident, the fact of her adoption. A teacher had assigned the fifth-grader the task of developing a family tree. Young Cherisse dutifully pulled out the family papers to research the names of great-grandparents and other relatives. A piece of paper caught her eye. It said she was adopted. No one had ever told her that.

"Mother?" she asked. "Am I really adopted?" Eilleen Thebeault, the woman Cherisse knew as "mother," told her the papers were not to be looked at. The two never talked about the matter again. "I did not want to hurt my mother," recalls Cherisse, "so I never said anything."

Stanley Thebeault, her adoptive father, also said nothing. He concentrated on developing skills as a jeweler and gemmologist, travelling to jobs across Canada and the U.S. as he rose in his trade. The family settled in Galveston, where Stanley opened Thebeault Jewelers downtown. They had finally arrived in the good life. Membership in the country club, Cherisse vying for the beauty queen title of Miss Shrimp Festival wearing a bathing suit and sash, the American dream. In 1972, the dream dies. Stanley Thebeault is shot to death in his Galveston store during a robbery attempt. The father might have told his daughter what he knew about the facts of her life once she became adult, but he never got the chance. Within five years, Eilleen succumbs after a long battle with cancer. Cherisse is orphaned again.

She spent some time at college, trained in law enforcement, no career really stuck, but when she met fireman Jim Combs she knew she was in love. Son Chuck was born in 1978, daughter Heather two years later. In 1986, Jim Combs dies fighting a blaze. From country club to single mother in south Texas. Orphaned, orphaned again, and widowed. Alone, so terribly alone.

These, then, are the facts of Cherisse's life, told on the phone that first night. Brother Reid was eight years older, sent to a seminary school for boys when Cherisse was a toddler. Reid was in college while Cherisse grew up. The death of the parents removed the only bond between them. It was sad. That's the way things go sometimes.

It sounds like a bad movie, a two-hanky made-for-TV weeper. It does not get much more tragic than this. But this is not a movie. This is my sister. She hasn't told me to go away. We might develop a relationship.

If we like each other. If I can tolerate her. If she can tolerate me. Please don't let her be Klan.

We recount histories, of life, of adoption thoughts. Cherisse remarried last year. Her husband Robert is a good man. He's supported Cherisse's early attempts to conduct her own search for a past. She had seen families reunited on television talk shows, so she and Robert wrote to the producers of Oprah, Donahue, Sally Jesse Raphael, Jennie

Jones and the like. The only response was a note from Jennie Jones' staff apologizing for not being able to help, and including some contact addresses of adoption services. Just a few weeks earlier, Cherisse had written to the passive registry in her home province of Nova Scotia, supplying what information she knew and asking if anyone was looking for her.

My application to the same registry had been on file since 1986.

(As it turned out, clerks at the registry matched Cherisse's letter to mine a few weeks later, and eventually informed us by mail that a match had occurred. By then Cherisse and I had already met, but we thanked the registry for its efforts. Had my journalism friends from the CBC not taken the time and effort to trace misspelled names, we would have wound up contacting each other anyway. The time, it seems, was right.)

By now we are laughing, trading one-liners as we feel each other out. Cherisse would like to meet her mother. My mother. Our mother.

I don't know this person who is Cherisse Fowler, who is my sister. I don't know if she has the finesse and grace to understand the fears of this mother, her secrets. I haven't given this enough thought. Mo had feared her son would show up one day and ruin her life by exposing her past. The fear was unfounded, but Mo did not know that then. Now, this instant, speaking on the telephone with Mo's first daughter, I share this fear. I don't know if Cherisse will bide her time or if she intends to board the next flight to Mo's home town and show up at her door. I don't know if she'll hang up from me and phone Mo and tell her to make room for one more. I don't know if she's thinking of extorting money to keep the secret.

For more than a year I've been talking on radio and television and in newspapers and magazines of how the secrecy must stop. Of how adult adoptees have a fundamental right to the facts of their lives. Now, this instant, on the telephone, I decide that I, too, will perpetuate the secrecy, for now at least. I will not tell this woman who is my sister where and how she can contact her mother. There are times, some say, that hypocrisy is justified. I wonder: is this one of those times? I will play the trick of giving her some information, a sop — like the authorities give adoptees — and play for time. The truth, but not the whole truth. That will have to wait while I play judge and jury, deciding for an adult human being what she may or may not know about herself. I am my mother's keeper. At least the keeper of her secrets. I am ashamed. The day I contacted my mother, I began to plot. The day I contacted my sister, I began to evade.

Cherisse is hungry for facts. Ravenous. I offer a few tempting morsels: first names, home towns, a reminder of the time when pregnancy equalled sin and shame, brief life histories — mere appetizers. Nothing that would allow even a skilled investigator to track the person down.

"I don't want to do anything to hurt her," says Cherisse. "She's been through enough already. But I'd like to meet her, of course. What do you think I should do?"

We've known each other for less than an hour. Already I'm playing the role of protective son, and now a brother being asked for advice. I like this role. I like this woman, I think. We will get to know each other, perhaps.

That's when the awful understanding hits. Until now I've operated from a one-sided vision: whether we two orphans develop a relationship depends solely on whether this unknown Cherisse is the type of person that I, in my arrogance, demand her to be. If she in any way fails to live up to my expectations, I will proceed no further.

For the first time it occurs to me to wonder: what happens if she doesn't like me?

Eight

What if my sister is scared of me?

For all she knows, I am a con man setting her up for extortion or trickery. A child molester, perhaps, just trying to get close to her kids. Maybe she's thinking I'm mentally disturbed, living constantly in the past, totally hung up on the issues of my birth. Or just a plain old ordinary loser who she'd rather not have in her family. Anyway, it's best not to hope for too much. She could still be Cherisse the Ku Klux Klansman or religious fanatic.

It is the morning after first contact. First contact. It sounds like an alien encounter. In a way, it is. We are alien to each other. Products of the same womb, the same genes, but products too of different nations, different backgrounds, different educations, different parents. Our pains and joys, our entire lives have been experienced separately. The fundamental fabric of our beings, the people we are today, was formed thousands of kilometers apart. We are each other's unknown, and the unknown, deep inside in the child part of our soul, is always a scary thing. Grown-ups call it xenophobia. Kids call it the bogey man. We are the bogey men, bogey brother and sister, bogey children.

Unlike the first phone call with Mo, where there was fear and secrecy and codes and hiding, this time there is openness. We have nothing to hide from the world. There is no shame from our births. A generation ago — Mo's time — there would have been cover stories. The A word was never mentioned. Today, a raft of words beginning with A are the stuff of afternoon TV talk shows, said loud and proud.

And what do I want out of this, anyway? For sixteen years, the fact that I have an older sister loomed large at times, scarcely mattered at others. Yesterday that fact became a name and a location and a voice on the phone with a history and a present. Now I know. I know who she is, and where she is. Now she knows who I am. Now this is no longer about just one person. About me. My search. My question. Now that question is answered, but in doing so, a whole other set of questions are posed. For sixteen years my search has been about self-centred, ego-centric me. By opening a door into the past, a whole other human being has been invited into my life.

Again.

I didn't even think about issuing that invitation. Now that I've found "my" sister, it also means she has found "her" brother. Do I really want to be someone else's possession? This is a question I should have thought about before tracking this Cherisse person down. Now, whether Rick likes it or not, this orphan game is no longer being played by just one set of rules. My rules. There's a whole other person involved now. Now it's "us," a brother and sister, joined by bonds of blood, connected by hitherto unknown parents.

I wonder if we'll like "us."

I will show this unknown sister who I am. Or, at least, who I want her to think I am. I gather documents, travel to a shop with a color photocopier to make copies of a magazine article I wrote about finding Mo, and a copy of my only photograph of our mother. I've told Cherisse on the telephone how I found her, but it is a lot of information for her to take in at one time, coupled with the emotional overload of finally learning the facts of her life. There is no way to know how much of the story she has already taken in, so I will send a care package of printed material to allow her to follow the story through at her own speed. The plan is twofold: as well as supplying her with information about her background, I will tell her about myself, hoping that the bylined print stories and book will cause her to think that her brother is a pretty nifty big-deal journalist.

Unlike Mo, who knew she had a son, Cherisse has never known of my existence. Perhaps has never even speculated about the existence of a full sibling. She might demand proof, and the fact that a national magazine has carried my story, accompanied by a two-page photograph of her brother Rick looking pensive and smoking a cigarette, should help convince her of my sincerity and the truth of my story.

I include a photocopy of a *TV Guide* profile of her brother, which claimed that "few informed viewers would doubt that CBC NewsCentre's Rick Ouston is the best journalist working in Vancouver's electronic media today." Okay, so the writer's job was to create fluff pieces and not look for dirt about Rick the reporter, and it does look like her brother is bragging, but an endorsement from *TV Guide* has got to go a long way in media-mad USA, and if she thinks me a braggart, well, at least she'll know her brother has something to brag about.

The accompanying letter begins: "It's not often that I'm at a loss for words. Today is one of those times. I've known of your existence for sixteen years, since I first applied for the information the adoption authorities would give me, so-called 'non-identifying information,' which mentioned that, oh, by the way, you've got a sister.

"Now that I've found you … where does one begin?" I describe myself, the search process, and just in case my sister-by-birth is a raving right-wing nutbar, the letter includes the note that "In the U.S., I'd be classified as a liberal, I guess. Strong views against racism, sexism and homophobia, and a supporter of health and welfare safety nets for those who need them." If we're going to discover we're incompatible, best we discover that now.

And, finally: "What do I want from all this? Can't think of anything, really. You had a right to know about your background. I'd like to sit down with you and talk into the night. We might become friends. Who knows. But if you're willing to give it a try, I am too.

"Take care

"Rick Ouston"

The sign-off takes some thought. "Sincerely" is too formal, but it's far too early to even think of signing off with "love," or even "affection." I don't know this person. Maybe a fondness will develop between us, maybe we'll become bitter enemies, maybe nothing will happen at all. Even signing off with "Your brother" is presumptuous. She might not want a brother. She's already got one, and he lost track of her. "Take care" sounds safe. And I sign my full name. We're not on first-name basis yet. We're not on any basis yet. I wonder if she'll think I'm too formal. Or if all the stories, books and documents with my name on them are too egocentric. I wonder. I wonder.

The package is sent by overnight courier. In Texas, Cherisse would recall later, she took it to her bedroom, opened the envelope, and cried. Her children wanted to see the contents of the envelope. Cherisse told them to go away.

I phone the next day. A girl's voice answers.

"No, my momma's not home," she drawls.

"Can you tell her Rick Ouston phoned, and ask her to call me," I say, preparing to hang up. I have nothing to say to a child.

"Are you my momma's brother?" she asks.

"Yes."

"Wow. I'm Heather. It's really freaky talking to you."

I have to stop and puzzle out the words. It sounds like she said "rilly fricky." I don't know what that means. Oh. Really freaky. She is a child. She gets her vocabulary from *Beverly Hills 90210*. She is a child whose mother has had no relatives, until now. There have never been phone calls from her mother's side of the family. Until now. Cherisse had said something about how she and the kids had lost track of Jim's family, but I wasn't sure what it meant. Today, right now, this little girl is talking to the first relative she's ever talked to. I am a stranger to her. I am an uncle to her.

Heather says her momma's been happy this past year, married to a good man who gave rings to her children during the ceremony and married them too. They escaped the crime and poverty of Galveston last year, moving to Robert's home town and joining his extended family of relatives and friends.

"Momma's gone to meet daddy at the oil fields. I don't know when she'll be back. She usually gets lost. Are you gonna come down and visit us?"

Yes, I say. "I'm looking forward to it."

"Me too."

Cherisse calls back later that night. Yes, she is happy now.

For many years, though, for too many years, there were the alone times. Widowed at 32, with Chuck and Heather barely out of diapers. Without enough skills to earn a decent wage. Never anything for extras, never time for

fun or for pleasure. Parents dead, brother away and un-
heard from. Alone, and broke. There was that Christmas
when all three of them were reduced to living in one little
room and if it wasn't for the friend bringing a tree, nothing
in the room would have indicated it was supposed to be
the festive season. There were trips to food banks and
social services, pleading to society to at least treat her
family like human beings, with some compassion. When
you're a single mother with a bad job and two kids, there's
not much else to do at night but sit, and be alone.

A disconnection from the rest of the world, made worse
by death and by poverty. And, on top of it all, the whispered fact of her own adoption meant that even the Thebeault relatives back in Nova Scotia weren't really her
relatives. Not truly.

She is looking forward to meeting me. We say our good-
byes. She says: "I love ya."

I say: "I love you, too." It is hard to say the words.
Hard because, again, it is a lie. To Mo, it is a lie when I
say I love you. To Cherisse it is too. I don't know this
person. How can I love her? How can I love them? How
can they say "I love you," when they don't know me? Is
there something about mothers which allows them to use
the word "love" so indiscriminately?

I have a sister.
Her name is Cherisse.
She lives in Texas.
She says she loves me.

New facts, and they repeat again and again like a mantra in my brain. Like the Hare Krishna chant or the
extended "Om" of meditationalists, the words bubble, pop,

and bubble again. Sister, Cherisse, Texas, love. Sister, Cherisse, Texas, love.

In 1974 she was a fact on a piece of paper. Today it is 1992, and my travel agent has booked a flight to Texas. The earliest flight she can get me on is September 10th. The date happens to be my birthday. I will arrive on my 37th birthday, to spend it with a sister I have never known.

The trip means an unplanned absence from a new job. Helen Slinger and I are working together again. This time we're producing an ancient CBC Television network show called *Front Page Challenge*, sort of *Meet the Press* meets *What's My Line*: part game show — Guess That Story — and part interview with a news maker. Helen is senior producer, long-time colleague Cameron Bell is executive producer. Cameron ran Vancouver's top-rated television newscast for twenty years or so, and we mused and sang over beers at the Press Club for the last ten of those years. Because of my stutter, I was one of the few journalists in Vancouver who had never asked Cameron for a job. A newspaper strike in 1984 changed that. I was recently divorced, broke, and asked Cameron if there was a spot available on his BCTV *NewsHour* as a writer or researcher, something that I could do without embarrassing both of us by trying to talk on TV. Cameron said he'd hire me, but only as an on-camera reporter. You'll be sorry, I said, but it worked out. Now we work together again, and just three weeks into the season I'm taking an unscheduled long weekend to visit my sister in Texas who I didn't know at the start of the season. Helen and Cameron are veteran journalists, accustomed to digesting new information quickly, accommodating it to make room for the next fact. They can live without me for the Texas trip.

The new job also offers an excuse for a smash-and-grab

visit of three days and two nights. "I've just got time for a long weekend," I tell Cherisse on the phone. In reality, I could take a week or more. But that could mean being stuck in a nothing town with people I don't like. Just in case, I check the schedule of the Toronto Blue Jays. On my birthday weekend they're playing the Rangers in Arlington. If the first meeting goes badly, I can always go home a day early, re-route the return flight schedule and catch a ball game with my favorite team. The trip wouldn't be a total loss.

Helen takes me shopping. I've been wearing jeans and T-shirts the past few years, letting my hair grow, a fashion statement of rebellion against years of TV hair and suits. But I don't want this new sister to think her brother is a slob. So today we're shopping for silk shirts, casual slacks. If clothes make the man then this man wants to make himself look financially successful, at least middle class. I might not like the strangers in Texas, but I want them to like me. Or at least not to dislike the stranger in their midst because he's wearing funny clothes. We giggle, Helen and I, two old friends, dressing up Rick for the big day. It feels like Christmas. Nice gift, a family, for the man who has everything but. The last trip to see family was clandestine, like a spy operation or tawdry sexual affair. No secrets this time, no stealthy, tricky sneaking around. My visit to see Mo had been cheapened by the deception. This time, we would meet openly. No shame, nothing to hide.

Except, maybe, the fact that my sister's new brother has no fashion sense.

Vancouver to Seattle to San Jose to Midland-Odessa International Airport. It is called an international airport because flights occasionally come in all the way from Mexico, just a few kilometers to the south. My travel agent has booked a room in the best motel in town. One of only three motels in town. It's not much of a town, she warned. And not much of a motel. But a room to myself is important. Cherisse and her family offered to put me up during the stay. Young Chuck can sleep on the couch.

"I don't want to put you out," I respond. In truth, I don't want to be stuck in a house 24 hours a day for three days and two nights with a bunch of banjo-playin' inbred Southern crackers. I saw *Deliverance*. Mrs. Ouston didn't raise no fool for a son. And anyway, Cherisse has said her county is dry. As in, no liquor for sale. It's a holdover from the old Women's Christian Temperance Union days. In reality, the ban-the-booze movement was based less on Jesus and more on the knowledge that liquor helped fuel wife beating and deadbeat dads who'd rather loaf and spend their money on shots and a beer instead of food. The adherents of Carrie Nation were arguably the continent's first successful feminists, and deserve deep admiration for their efforts.

But this is 1992. I pride myself on being at least egalitarian when it comes to gender politics, but when it comes to having a nightcap, no granddaughter of a Prohibitionist is going to stand in my way. A room of my own means a place to stash a duty-free bottle of scotch, to smoke and drink in private without offending the sensibilities of people who are strangers.

The rental car is waiting at the airport. While filling out the interminable forms, I tell the clerk the reason why a Canadian is visiting the deep South.

"Just like on Oprah!" she says in the slow and broad twang of West Texas, the accent that first caused me to believe that Cherisse's new husband contravened the dry laws of her county. Down here, west of the heart of Texas, talk may not be cheap, but it sure is slow.

North by north-west, then, from Midland-Odessa International Airport, in a rented white Toyota along two-lane paved roads that cut through land flat and deserted. It could be a prairie road in Manitoba, the kind that stretch forever and look like they go nowhere. I have driven roads like this many times. Alone, mostly, like this evening. Feeling comfortable, being alone. What's it going to be like, I wonder, not being alone anymore? The sun is setting, twilight, the air perfumed with the stink of oil wells along state highway 1788. It is getting darker and I wish it wasn't. I don't know where I'm going and I don't know what will happen when I get there. At the very least I'd like to be able to see along the way. The rent-a-car map shows a left turn onto highway 176 and there is Andrews, Texas, the corner of Main and Broadway. In cities, a corner called Main and Broadway suggests big times, bright lights, commercial action. In cities, Main and Broadway would be a big deal. In Andrews, Texas, Main and Broadway is dust and a few old buildings. There is still time to catch that ball game.

The motel clerk smiles and studies my American Express card and says: "Your sister phoned. Y'all supposed to call her."

Cherisse answers the phone and we arrange for her and Robert to come to the motel; I will follow them in the rental car to their home. The car is an escape clause, just in case. In case of what, I don't know.

Inside the room, pacing, like the time waiting for Mo. The motel television carries the usual networks and HBO so at least there's a movie channel that I can watch if I'm stuck in a room until escaping to the ball game.

Knocking, on the motel door. This is it then. Open the door.

Two people stand outside. The man is young, smiling,

mid-twenties maybe, short hair. The woman is short, glasses, jeans and a T-shirt, hair pulled back in a ponytail, long and thick and dark brown. Her nose is mine. Her jaw is, too. It's a bit unsettling. Imagine a picture of yourself, altered by computer graphics a bit to change the gender, just a little nip here and tuck there and voila! you are not the man or woman you saw in the mirror that morning. You are, instead, someone else, metamorphosed into a different sex, but still you. This is what brothers and sisters must see in each other all the time, and it's no big deal. The only time I've ever seen it is in Mo, but she's a lot older. This is my sister. So this is how it feels.

Like Mo, Cherisse takes the initiative. She walks forward a couple of steps, looks up, into a face she doesn't know. It makes me feel tall. Like Mo, she spreads her arms and comes closer and I open mine and move closer and we hug, tight. I can't think of words to say. Mothers know how to hug. She is a mother, my sister, and she knows.

The man, it must be Robert, the husband, smiles and raises a compact camera to his eye. A flash goes off. So he is the kind of person who would interrupt a special moment like this with the cheap intrusiveness of a snapshot.

I am glad. I hope the photo turns out well. With Mo, I was afraid to take photographs, afraid of making her afraid that the photographic evidence could be used against her.

Cherisse nestles her face into my shoulder. I clutch her back, ending up with a handful of ponytail, thick and soft. She has a lot of hair. A hair fixation, likely. Just like me. Just like her brother. She wears glasses; I can feel the frames digging uncomfortably into my neck. She wears glasses, like her brother. I am worried Robert the husband might take offence at this clutching of his southern belle.

But he stands smiling, in the doorway, holding back, letting his wife take the time she wants.

In 1974, barely a man, hardly an adult, a piece of paper told me I have a sister. Today I am twice as old as I was then, and the sister is no longer typewritten information on a piece of paper. She is real, human, short, warm, holding me and I am holding her and we are orphans and we are orphans no longer.

Finally we let go and look at each other.

"Wow," I say. It is the only word I can think of saying.

"Yeah," she says, smiling, half laughing. "Wow."

*T*he streets of Andrews are quiet. Smallville, U.S.A. The Fowler house is nondescript, a tad rundown, blending with the neighborhood. No one passing by would know that inside, brother and sister are getting to know each other for the first time.

Cherisse's children are asleep. Thanks to God herself for small mercies. During the years my stories have angered serial killers, Nazi war criminals, pimps, Klansmen, organized gangsters, bikers and con men. None of them scare me more than having to make small talk with children. In the past few years, friends have had children and I have grown to know them and even not dislike them, but their numbers are few. Unknown children fill me with dread. I don't know what to say to them.

The kids are asleep, it's my birthday, and there's nobody jumping out from behind couches for a surprise party. This is good. It has been some years since I've celebrated this day. Reporting and teaching and public speaking place me at centre stage often enough — I don't need birthday parties. I enjoy celebrating other people's birthdays, but not mine. The past few days I've lived in fear that Cherisse and Robert would feel a need to throw a surprise party to mark the day, but instead, things are perfect. The house is silent. The kids are asleep, and there's a half-dozen Corona in the fridge.

Cherisse opens one, rams a wedge of lime down its neck and asks: "Would you like a beer?"

"Yes. Please. A lot. I mean, not a lot of beer, but thanks a lot. When you said this was a dry county, I thought that meant dry, totally."

Our first conversation, live and in person, and it revolves around booze. She is truly her brother's sister.

It turns out that although the sale of bottled alcohol is prohibited for fifty miles around, there is no prohibition against importing potables into the county for personal consumption. The nearest liquor store is twelve miles away, straight down the freeway past the county line. Cherisse was there this morning. She lights up a cigarette, smiles a bit shamefacedly and says: "When I saw that picture of you in the magazine, smoking that cigarette, I thought: 'Oh thank God! He's a smoker!'"

Robert sits with us at the kitchen table. He is still smiling, and he looks at his watch and says it's late, I'll be going to bed soon. Without using words he's said: It's okay, Rick. This is your time, yours and Cherisse's. I'm not going to interfere. I'll be gone soon.

He is a southern gentleman, this man who I first thought a drunk and a fool. I am ashamed to have thought those thoughts.

Cherisse wants to hear again how she was found. She knows the story already, but this is the history we have so far, like old family tales that get told and retold during Christmas dinners and anniversaries, the stories that get told about favorite aunts and long-dead relatives, handed down, family stories. We have just one story to share so far, and there is so much to know and learn that it's comfortable to start off telling each other something we already know. Mostly, she wants to hear about Mo, about her mother, about our mother.

I recount everything I know, except for last names and the town in which she lives. Not being evasive this time. Instead, being honest, telling Cherisse that her mother's secrets remain secrets, and that her son has promised not to expose her.

(I still don't trust you, Cherisse, even though I know your face now and have held you. I don't trust you. You might drink another beer and decide to phone your mother and announce yourself to her family and demand a daughter's due. Maybe you deserve that right. It's not for me to say you don't. But I can't trust you. Not yet.)

She understands. She doesn't push for specifics, I don't offer. We sketch brief family histories, marriages, hers, mine. The photo album that was assembled for Mo is in my suitcase, and we flip through pictures. Cherisse pulls out stacks of photos, the Thebeaults, Reid and Stanley and Eilleen, baby Cherisse and Cherisse growing up, at school, as Miss Thebeault Jewelers vying for the Shrimp Festival title, a first brief marriage to a man her mother said she shouldn't marry, and her mother turned out to be right. Later, her marriage to Jim Combs, baby pictures of Chuck and Heather, an absence of pictures where photographs should be of Chuck and Heather growing up but there wasn't enough money to pay for photos.

Tonight is the night to start to know each other, for each of us to learn about the other. For me it's time to determine what the awful truths are, if there are indeed awful truths to learn. The Blue Jays play ball tomorrow, and if this blood relative is someone I don't want to know, my bag is already packed. Whether she knows it or not, Cherisse is being tested to see if her brand-new brother thinks her a lout. A sort of sibling pop quiz: okay class, you weren't expecting one, but here it is, ten questions, you've got a half hour to prove whether you're worthy.

First up, homophobia. I tell her about Lorraine, and it feels funny talking about a sister who isn't to a sister who wasn't. Even the word, sister, feels awkward. Lorraine is my sister, always has been for what it was worth, and until the past year it wasn't worth much. But this past year a bond has been created, cemented out of trust and honesty, and if this new sister shows hatred or hostility toward my old sister because of the reality of her sexual orientation, then she'll lose.

She passes. Like her brother, Cherisse hasn't given the issue of homosexuality a lot of thought. She has friends who are, men and women, but the whys and wherefores just haven't been a priority. Her grasp on the issues of alternative sexuality sounds a tad naive, based on office gossip and TV talk shows, but we wrestle through the differences between transsexualism and transvestism, between stereotypes of bull-dykes and lipstick lesbians, me easily falling into didacticism, Cherisse playing the role of eager and willing student. At least on this topic. She listens as her brother talks of what he has learned, and she does not argue and quote the Bible. There are more cigarettes and more beer as we sit at the kitchen table the same way Lorraine and I have sat at kitchen tables, talking into the night after everyone else has gone to bed.

Talk turns to other minorities, the treatment of native Indians in Canada and the U.S., the natives of New Mexico whose border is just 60 miles to the west. Cherisse is angry at the way white immigrants stole the land of the natives, both in her adopted country and in her home and native land. Cherisse explains that Robert's mother worked as a teacher on reserves in New Mexico for many years, that Robert grew up among natives and has taught his wife about their values and injustices and a culture hovering on annihilation.

She hasn't flinched at my criticism of the U.S. for funding the Contras in Nicaragua, or the fact that I reported from that country during its phony civil war in 1984, where I saw first hand the democratically elected Sandinista government forced to fight against U.S.-supplied arms while its economy lay in ruins. She's not a my-country-right-or-wronger like her mom, and she lost too many old high school friends in Vietnam but does not blame the Vietnamese. We drink, smoke, discover that we share similar politics. We are strangers, but this doesn't feel strange. It feels right.

Turns out that Robert, too, was adopted, sort of. His parents divorced when he was a child, and his mother eventually remarried an Andrews widower named David Fowler. David had three kids from his first marriage, and adopted young Robert and his sister Carrie as his own, giving them his name. Now Robert's mother is dead, and David remarried again, this time to a single woman who had a daughter. The Fowlers are accustomed to blended families and that's why they made Cherisse feel so much at home. Robert had also encouraged his wife to seek out her history. In fact, days after his first phone call to Vancouver, Robert wrote a letter to the editor of the twice-a-week Andrews County *News* to encourage other adoptees to find their pasts.

"My wife and her children, whom I proudly call my own, have no family to speak of," he wrote, outlining Cherisse's new discovery. "My wife now has a sense of who she is. Some of the who's, how's, why's have been answered.

"She now has a brother who wants to know, and have

someone to care for — a sister. They have a lot of years to make up.

"The only thing a loving husband can do is make sure she has the opportunity to make up those years with her brother, and she will.

If there were one line to summarize the story, he said, it is: "Good things come to those who wait patiently — my wife's wait is over!"

Robert Fowler's letter prompted the paper to write a feature story on Cherisse and her new brother, complete with photograph of the Fowler family holding the magazine picture of her brother smoking his face off. The past week, said Cherisse, it felt like everyone in town had stopped to ask if she was the woman who had found her brother. She enjoyed the media spotlight. Like brother, like sister, like brother-in-law, an extended family of media sluts.

The Blue Jays will have to play without me.

But what about Mo?

In the U.S. Midwest, a housewife and mother is going about her housewifely and motherly duties the same as she has for more than 30 years. For all those years she has kept her secrets to herself. Tonight she has no way of knowing that those secrets are sitting around a kitchen table, swapping stories, trading lives, getting to know each other. Her secret daughter and her secret son are enjoying each other's company. Usually parents of adult children like it when their kids sit around and talk like old friends. Usually aging parents can sit to one side or lie in their beds in satisfaction, congratulating themselves for raising children who can communicate with each other, who love each other, who will watch out for each other. But in this case the parent is thousands of miles away and does not have a clue that the children she bore in secrecy and in shame are sitting together, discussing what to do about mom. Like children since the beginning of time, we begin to plot about our mother, about ways to manipulate her, about the best way to approach her to tell her something she doesn't necessarily want to know. That we have found each other.

It has been months since Mo phoned last. Tonight the telephone might ring at my home in Vancouver, Mo sneaking away from her husband to telephone her son collect so her shame will not show up on a telephone bill. Tonight, if she phones, there will be no one to respond. The answering machine will click on and my recorded voice will ask the caller to please leave a message after the tone. The operator will tell my mother there is no answer. If Mo phones tonight, she will think her son is out, perhaps partying, perhaps working.

There will be no way for our mother to know that we know who we are.

*B*ack at the motel room, it is late, a two-hour time-zone difference and twelve hours of airplanes and airports and hours of talking with a stranger who is a stranger no more. Maybe it is the length of the day, fear of the unknown, the effects of the beer, relief, or all of the above. Whatever the reason, I cry, alone in the motel room. Just a few seconds, a couple of muffled whimpers, but enough of a release.

Even now, writing this, I can't quite figure out why the tears. Tears have never come easy. As an adult, the only tears I've shed have been upon getting dumped. There was some mist when it looked like E.T. was dead, but that was rare. Tears of joy? The phrase gets used a lot, but until now it's always rung false to my ears. Maybe this time, though. Just maybe.

Whatever the reason, the tears flush out the tension of the day and sleep comes easy.

The next day, back to Cherisse's house. Young Heather is pleading illness, likely feigned, and staying home for ministrations of chicken soup, daytime TV and interrupting her mother and new-found uncle whenever they start discussing what to do about their mother.

Chuck, fourteen, comes home after school. His mother has gone to the store. I am home alone, with the kids. A kid who is a stranger, although we share a genetic heritage. The biological relation isn't helping. Chuck does not know me. I don't want to impose on him. I remember being a fourteen-year-old boy, dumb as a sack of hammers, believing the world revolved around my tiny self, and looking for a reason, any reason, to rebel. Chuck is nephew to my uncle, but this is Chuck's world that I'm invading. I don't want to interfere with his world.

"Hi," I say, smiling my best pretending-to-be-a-grownup smile, reaching out a hand for a manly handshake, firm but not too firm. "I'm Rick." Not Uncle Rick. That would be imposing, forcing a relationship he may not want. Just Rick.

We make small talk, very teeny tiny small talk about high school football and Canada and Galveston and the heat of the desert here in Andrews — some weather, eh? — and after about a thousand days or so Cherisse comes back home and finally there's a real adult back in the house.

Chuck becomes silent, watching some dreck on television, then turns to me and says: "Uh, Rick?" in a drawl made even slower by hesitance. He is unsure whether he should say what he is going to say next. "Uh, would y'all mind if we'all called y'all Uncle Rick?"

Another smile, genuine this time, and another feeling of being a twit.

"I'd be honored, Chuck."

Cherisse and her family treat me like you would treat any guest. A drive around the streets of Andrews — there aren't many streets — dinner at a Mexican restaurant — there aren't much of any other kind — and take in the high-school football game. The Permian Basin region of Texas is famous for its high-school football, subject of the bestseller *Friday Night Lights* by Pulitzer Prize-winner H.G. Bissinger. It is literally the social event of the week. In a county of barely 10,000, at least 6,000 are at the stadium tonight, cheering on a bunch of pimply faced boys. The marching band performs a rendition of Billy Ray Cyrus's "Achy Breaky Heart," a tune sitting on the number one spot of the country music hits for the last several months. I have read of the song's popularity, but had never heard it. Tonight, for the first time, "Achy Breaky Heart," with trombones. Cheerleaders perform the complicated choreography that got them to the state finals this year. It is indeed a different world from mine. It is the world of my sister. Cherisse and Robert usually volunteer with the Jay-Cees for football night, selling pop and hot dogs, raising money for the town's charities. Tonight, though, Cherisse gets the evening off so she can parade her brother around. She introduces me to several score of the local townsfolk, all of whom have read the newspaper account and who want to meet the brother from up there in Canada.

It is a Fowler family tradition on football Friday nights to repair after the game to the home of David, Robert's adoptive father. Tonight will be no different, just a regular Friday. It is also tradition at David Fowler's to drink something he calls "candy." It is a combination of bourbon and cola, poured over ice into an insulated foam drinking container from a convenience store, sort of a Big Gulp for people who don't like their livers. Pour bourbon to the count of seven, top up with Pepsi, cloying but addictive.

Minutes after I remark that the football game was the first time I'd heard "Achy Breaky Heart," a relative has picked up a Billie Ray Cyrus video from her home and now it's plugged into David's VCR. Of course there's a television set beside the hot tub, and we sit, Cherisse and Rick and David and a coming-and-going of other relatives, our eyeglasses steaming from the swirling waters, our drink glasses draining, under the Texas moon. I have known these people for fewer than 24 hours. Already they are family.

David's wife Shirley, a nurse at Permian General Hospital, is working tonight and can't be home to greet the new addition to her extended family. But she has left a treat. Knowing that Cherisse's brother was arriving on his birthday, she baked a cake, decorating it with yellow icing in the shape of a bunch of bananas. There is writing on the cake, in icing as well.

"Happy birthday, Rick," it says. "Welcome to the bunch."

There are too many children around to afford much time for talk between newfound brother and sister. Instead, we peer at each other through fog-shrouded glasses, grinning.

Children occupy much of the following day, demanding attention and stories and whatever it is that children need. Cherisse wants to talk about what she should do about Mo — write her a letter, perhaps, that I could forward — but there are children and dogs and cats and neighbors and little time to plot or plan. She doesn't ask for her mother's last name, or the place where she lives. Instead, she asks me to tell her everything I know, have heard and have seen about Mo, seeing her mother through the eyes of her brother. She listens to tales of phone calls, of our meeting at the Holiday Inn, the sketchy details that I know of our genetic heritage.

"I want to meet her one day, Rick. Like you did. Just

to see her and to touch her. But I don't want to wreck her life," says Cherisse. She listens to the story of Roger the husband, and shakes her head.

We fantasize about Mo taking her husband aside, about a conversation that would go something like this:

"Roger, remember a couple of years ago when I told you I'd had a son before I met you? Yeah, Rick, that's right. Well, it slipped my mind at the time, but, ha ha, well, I had a daughter the year before him. Yeah, I guess I forgot to tell you. Isn't that funny?"

We agree that Roger would likely not see the humor in that.

I am embarrassed to tell Cherisse about my last conversation with our mother, the one in which I asked her to cut down on the phone calls. Since that time, I hadn't heard from her. For all I knew, she might have died since then. But at least I had her phone number and address. If need be, I could phone her home without identifying myself and use my sneaky reportorial skills to make sure she hadn't moved.

We settle on a plan of sorts. Cherisse will write a letter to her mother and send it to me. I'll forward it to Mo in an envelope without any return address. It's a bit of a gamble — it is Roger's habit, she'd said, to pick up the mail each day — but it would be a gamble worth taking. If Roger asked about the letter, she could toss it off as a boring letter from a long-forgotten relative that he wouldn't be interested in.

A brother and sister, plotting ways around our mother's husband. Plotting, as kids have plotted forever against their parents. We feel like kids, Cherisse and I, capturing a bond we'd never shared. We sit at the kitchen table, giggling about ways to avoid the evil Roger.

Our last night together in Texas ends up at the Moose

Lodge, a private club for members only. Outwardly a social club, inside the Moose Lodge's locked doors a five-piece country and western band has the crowd line-dancing, drinks are served from two bars, folks play pool and shuffleboard. So much for this dry county. But, Robert explains, all liquor bought must be consumed on the premises and, after all, admission to the club is exclusively for members only.

Membership is restricted to those who want to belong.

Cherisse attempts to teach her little brother the Texas two-step, and he is embarrassed when he steps on her toes. Another dance involves groups of people linking arms around shoulders and yelling "Bullshit!" at times in the song that I can't quite figure out, but the beer is cold, these are real live Texans that are teaching the intricacies of the Boot-Scootin' Boogie, and a man who says his name is Chester is buying beer at the bar.

Not a bad evening.

We close the bar, herd out to the parking lot. Robert is the designated driver and has spent the night drinking Cokes with his best friend and former Coast Guard buddy Richard, a barrel-chested Mexican who married his high school sweetheart Bonnie and started having kids when she was sixteen. We've spent the night shooting pool, smoking cigarettes, swapping jokes and laughs, and Bonnie watched from the corner of her eyes the several times that I deflected attempts at racist jokes from David, Robert's adoptive father. My criticism of the jokes hasn't bothered David any, but Bonnie smiled each time, shyly. Out in the parking lot, the heat of the desert day has evaporated, replaced by a chill black night scented with the last hay of the season.

Richard extends his hand, takes mine.

"You know, I was going to say it was good meeting

you, and you take care of yourself. But, now that I've gotten to know you, let me say this: *Hasta luega, amigo.*"

"See you later, friend." It sounds a bit like John Wayne trying not to be mushy. It also sounds genuine.

The flight back to Vancouver leaves at eight o'clock the next morning. That means getting up at five, just a couple hours away. There is no time for more talk of what to do about Mo. Robert drives us back to the motel. They will drop me off, go home to their lives, me to mine. It has been a very long weekend.

In front of the motel door, Cherisse opens her arms for a hug and we clasp, tight. The face that looks like mine turns upward, she looks into my eyes and says: "I love you."

A moment's pause.

I say: "I love you back."

The words are genuine. The emotion sincere.

Cherisse climbs back into the car, closes the door, then snuggles into Robert's shoulder. She is not fast enough to hide the tears. They drive away, through the parking lot, onto the highway, the tail lights grow tiny, then are gone.

In the motel room I pour a drink. Light a cigarette.

And again, I cry.

Not much, just a couple of chest heaves and sniffle or two. But it is enough.

Nine

Two weeks after the weekend in Texas, I took the ferry to Vancouver Island for a couple of days' bacchanalia at my sister Lorraine's, partly because I wanted to see her and partly because I wanted her to see me as still being her brother despite the location and addition of Cherisse. Lorraine met me at the ferry, and on our way home we stopped at a shopping mall to pick up fourteen-year-old daughter Adrienne and her friend. Amidst small talk of school and travels and Texas, Adrienne turned to her young friend and said: "My Uncle Ricky found his real sister."

Thank God for straight lines, I thought.

"No, Adrienne. Your mom's my real sister," I said, giving Lorraine's shoulder a squeeze. She smiled, face scrunched self-deprecatingly, and all weekend told the story to friends and relatives. Our bond is strong because we have decided it will be strong.

Is that love? Perhaps. Is that the love that Mo has spoken of, and Cherisse, a love that is real because the person chooses it to be real? Should recipients of that love scrunch their faces up and look heavenward in feigned embarrassment? Why not? As long as the message they give is that they receive the love in trust and honor. I am learning to trust, and to be worthy of trust. I am learning to love.

Now, at home on weekend nights, late, alone, the phone refused to ring. There was no AT&T operator asking if I would accept a collect call from Mo. Her son wanted to tell his mother about these feelings of trust and love for his sisters, and he could not. I told the story of meeting Cherisse to Ann Ouston and sister Sharon, and their happiness at my peace of mind was visible. Sharon and I spent an afternoon together, the first in many years, and she finally agreed to register with adoption reunification organizations and begin her own search. My story was told to friends and co-workers, on radio and national television talk shows, and I couldn't tell the one person I wanted to tell.

I want my mommy.

Just to tell her that her son was happy. But the feeling of closure and connection — closure of that which was undone; connection to someone who before existed only as a sentence fragment in an anonymous report — went unshared. Listening endlessly to a mother professing love for the son she could not have twisted my guts; driving her away in a selfish bid for peace was driving me nuts. The phone refused to ring, sitting silent, mocking.

Also still silent was Michael, the unknown half brother who had never acknowledged my one and only letter. When the photographs from Texas were developed I sent him a print of Cherisse and me, with a note advising him that, by the way, you have yet another half sibling. "As near as I can tell, there aren't any other surprises for me to tell you about," the letter said.

Months later I had run into Dave Candow, the radio

producer from Newfoundland who first told me of Michael's existence. He'd recently been back to Newfoundland and had met Michael. They had talked about me, Candow said. Michael seemed pleased that I'd written. So Michael had received the first letter. But there had been no reply. Perhaps the photograph would prompt some action.

While the absence of word from Mo was hardly cause for joy, all this adoption stuff had at least offered a way around the annual horror of Christmas. This year I would go to Texas.

Christmas historically has not been my favorite time of year, no matter what Bing Crosby and his ilk say. As a child, too many years of being broke during the festive season had hardly offered cause for joy, and after Fred Ouston died we maintained the traditional tree and gifts and meals, but it felt hollow in his absence. It felt, in fact, as if we were pretending to be a family just to keep up appearances, conforming to societal pressures to make merry while feeling there was little to make merry about. Truly, his death had knocked the stuffing from the family he'd created with Ann, and those he left behind went through the motions because the calendar and the endless carols on AM radio said we should.

As a reporter, I'd made it a tradition to write or broadcast something "Christmassy" each year: sometimes a column which would conclude that things aren't so bad; sometimes a little slice-of-life reportage, seeing the festive season through the eyes of someone old remembering the days of their youth.

One December 23rd as a television reporter, I was

assigned to a story about a Vancouver restaurant called Kettle of Fish which was preparing to hold its annual free dinner for welfare families. It was something the restaurant's owners had done for years, quietly, with no fanfare. In the tell-it-with-pictures school of television journalism, my report should have ended with pictures of happy poor people chowing down on what was probably their only classy restaurant meal of the year. Instead, a few hours before meal-time, I sat down in front of the camera and spoke directly to the lens.

"We were going to stay here tonight and take pictures of the people having their meal," I said. "But then I remembered a Christmas, about 25 years ago, when my family was down on its luck. We had a visit that year from a Catholic charitable organization. They brought us money, and food, and when they left, we cried. Partly because it was Christmas and we now had enough to see us through. Partly because it was Christmas and we were broke and people knew it. Instead of meeting the people who come here tonight with cameras and lights, I thought it more in keeping with the spirit of the season, and of the gift, if they had their present in peace."

That's how the report ended, with my mug on the tube instead of pictures of the people the story was about. A gamble, unprofessionally unobjective, but the television station's switchboard jammed with callers congratulating us for not exploiting the plight of the poor, and dozens of viewers sent in cards and notes of thanks. It felt good to have stirred some warm and gooey feelings in the hearts of the public. Inside, however, my heart still felt cold, alone, like a little boy having a crummy Christmas.

For a few years there was Christmas with the family of my young wife, and I'd grown close and warm with her brothers and in-laws, but the marriage breakdown broke down those bonds too. When I could no longer use Wendy's family as an excuse to avoid spending Christmas with my own, I spent a decade begging off Ouston Christmas dinners by having to work that day in newsrooms. "News happens on Christmas too," I'd say. "The reporters who have kids, they should be allowed to get the day off."

"We understand," Ann and Sharon would say, and if they saw through my deceptions they never made mention. There'd been Christmas getaways and hideaways, going as far one year as taking the phone off the hook and locking myself into my apartment with a lover, a lot of food and too much wine. Last year I'd spent the hardly festive holiday with Lorraine as she went home to cook one last Christmas meal for family and friends. The strain over the overloaded table hung thicker than the odor of Brussels sprouts, as a husband and kids rent asunder by their mother's reality pretended that all was well. All was not well, and all were glad when the night was finished.

This year, Lorraine would have her girls over to her house for Christmas Day brunch and gifts, and the kids would spend the evening with their dad. This year, Lorraine was okay. Her brother's absence would not be an abandonment.

For Cherisse, it would be the first time in fifteen years she'd spent Christmas with a relative. It would be the first time in her life she d spend Christmas with a blood relative, not including her own children.

And it was her children, during the Christmas of 1992, who transformed this holiday season into a memorable one for their new uncle.

It happened on Christmas Eve, while Cherisse and Robert were busy wrapping presents in their bedroom. Toys and clothes and a typewriter and ghetto blasters, an assortment of gifts picked up during the year, intended to make their kids happy. They spent more than they could afford on Heather and Chuck, disregarding the family budget in favor of giving some joy to children who hadn't had many bountiful Christmases in their lifetimes. Both parents wielded scissors, hacking great chunks from rolls of wrapping paper, sticky-taping the ends together, heaping piles of gift-wrapped presents to one side of the bed and pulling yet more unwrapped treasures from closets and from under the bed. The wrapping process took at least three hours — we all knew that the unwrapping would take a few minutes.

As an observer, I couldn't help feeling the futility of all that work for such a short pay-off time. But Cherisse and Robert reveled in their job, giggling and smiling among ribbons and bows. They were doing what parents have done since Christmas became a tradition of giving — giving to their children, so the young ones would have some joy. Giving, and taking pleasure from it. At that moment, in a bedroom festooned with roll-ends of gift-wrap, I finally figured it out. Christmas is for children. Having never had any, I had remained stuck in perpetual adolescence, waiting my turn for peace and joy and goodwill to men. At least, to this man. A tiny epiphany, perhaps, for someone who has spent his life with his head firmly up his own butt. And perhaps a realization which would be dismissed as obvious by any parent. But for me, it transformed the horrible spirits of Christmases past into mere unrealistic expectations. Probably no one will ever note that, like Scrooge, from that day forward I knew how to keep Christmas well, if any man possessed the knowledge. But at least there would be no more locking myself away on December 25th and hiding from the light of children's eyes.

The night after Christmas, the adults packed themselves

into a van driven by Robert, the designated driver, and drove past the county line to a real live cowboy bar for an evening of tush-pushin', boot-scootin' and tequila-shootin'. Cowgirl wannabes in painted-on Levis, cowboy pretenders wearing dress-up shirts in west Texas Day-Glo colors. The bar housed about 500 of us, enticed by drinks for a buck and a chance to leave the kiddies behind. One can only take so much festive warm-and-fuzziness. And a few hours of line dancing helps to work off the candied-ham overload of the evening before.

Late in the evening, Cherisse stood before me and extended her hand to mine, tugging me to the dance floor. The song sounded like a slow waltz, and I was puzzled. We'd tried some sprightly two-stepping and basic rock'n'-roll dancing together, but this sounded like music for lov-ers wanting to hold each other tight. For me, it would be like kissing my sister. Or, at least, dancing with my sister.

Then I realized what Cherisse had done. She'd asked the deejay to play a song by Michelle Wright, a country singer from my home town who'd scored an international hit with a recording called "He Would Be Sixteen" — ostensibly a song from a woman who'd gotten pregnant as a young cheerleader and who had given the baby up for adoption sixteen years earlier.

Unknown to each other, we'd heard the song on our respective radios a few thousand miles apart, and both had taken the tune personally. There, on the dance floor, I held my sister tight, and she held me, and we swayed to the music, burying moist eyes into each other's shoul-der.

*C*all it karma, kismet or fate, I've believed none of it. Not until Billy Ray Cyrus changed all of our lives forever. It began with the letter Cherisse wrote to Mo. The letter arrived in Vancouver in the spring. I was to forward it to our mother.

"Dear Mo," the letter said, "My name is Cherisse Combs Fowler. I was born in Sydney, Nova Scotia, July 1, 1954. I was adopted by Stanley and Eilleen Thebeault. I know my given name was Rosilyn Griffin and that you are my mother."

It wasn't until reading her letter that I realized my sister did not know how to spell the name that had been hers — Rosalind. Her brother still knew more about her origins than she did.

Cherisse's letter sketched out her life and family in long hand, gently, trying not to frighten the woman who was our mother.

"I know reading this letter will be as hard for you to read as it is for me to write. I am afraid of making you afraid. I don't want to do anything to cause you grief, but now that I know who you are it would seem wrong not to let you know I'm OK and to thank you for giving me life." More family history, and an invitation: "You can write me or phone collect. I understand it would be late when you call. I think I understand the pressure you are under. I know whatever happens, we will never have a mother-daughter relationship. I don't expect one. I would still like to be able to know you and you me. I am waiting and hoping to hear from you."

Part of that plan involved my telephoning Mo and asking her to send me the address of a friend or business to which I could mail a letter without arousing Roger's suspicion. More than a year had passed since I'd last heard from Mo. Now it was time for me to phone her, clandestinely, conducting a one-sided conversation to try for a safe mailing address. If Mo wouldn't cooperate, I was prepared to mail the letter anyway, directly to her home in South Dakota.

I was not prepared to find that she had vanished.

The female voice that answered the phone call to Mo's telephone number said merely: "She doesn't live here anymore. She's gone."

"Gone? What do you mean, gone? Has something gone ... is she ... "

"No, she's not dead. She's moved."

"Do you know her new address?

"No, and I wouldn't give it to you if I did."

The woman thinks I'm some kind of a bill collector or something. Someone hunting Mo down as prey. Maybe she's right. I'm hunting for the birthright of my sister. The hunt has stopped. My mother is lost. Again.

She has abandoned her son. Again. It would appear she's not dead, but the directory assistance operator for the town she'd moved to a year earlier has no listing for Mo. Nor does the operator for Durango, where I'd first found her. She hadn't moved back. She'd moved away. And she hadn't told her son.

Maybe she didn't care. Maybe her son had frightened her off for good when he told her not to call so often. Maybe she thought her son was better off without her.

Now her son had a letter in his hand, a letter from her daughter, and didn't know what to do with it.

The first order of business was to tell Cherisse that her mother had moved. She deserved to know that much. And now that Mo had vanished, we agreed that my pledge to honor her anonymity was finished. She had dishonored her son; now he was prepared to break his personal pledge to protect her anonymity. I'd known where she was; I now knew no longer. I'd have to track her down all over again.

I went back to the file of documents I'd collected during the first search for Mo, and found her father's obituary, which contained the names of her brothers and sisters. The first time, I'd called a sister-in-law back in Newfoundland. She hadn't been suspicious then, but another call from someone with the same voice might cause her to wonder. This time I'd phone another name from the old newspaper clipping, once again acting jaunty, just a by-the-way-whatever-happened-to-Mo kind of call. And once again, a small-town woman rustled through some papers near her phone and offered the address of her sister. The woman never knew she was talking with a nephew she never even knew she had.

Mo's new home was in Montana. The long-distance operator offered a phone number under "Landon, Roger and Mo." Now it was done. It was out of my hands. Cherisse and I talked on the phone, and I gave her the secret of her mother's new home and last name. Cherisse would send her letter herself, directly, and we'd wait to find out what happened next. I returned the letter Cherisse had written to Mo, sending it back to Texas. Cherisse hadn't kept a copy, so it was quicker than trying to rethink what she'd already written.

The day after Cherisse received her letter back, a U.S. television network carried a one-hour special featuring country hunk Billy Ray Cyrus. Possessed of massive biceps, a passable voice and a hummable ditty called "Achy Breaky Heart," Billy Ray had dominated the country and western charts all year. The song received saturation air play, sold gazillions, won the hearts of country queens, and was easy to dance to. We'd watched Cyrus' video on my first trip to Texas, in the hot tub, had enjoyed the Andrews High School Band's arrangement of it during the football game, had even danced to it at the Moose Lodge, and watching his show, I thought of Cherisse in Texas. The show had undoubtedly been watched in the Fowler household two time zones ahead, so we might be connected by some achy breaky psychic energy. Or, at least, have watched something together so we'd have something to share in our next telephone call.

Midway through the broadcast, just about the time I started thinking I could use a break from Billy Ray, the phone rang.

"It's the Sprint operator," the voice said. "Would you accept a collect call from Mo?"

A tsunami of emotions: relief that she's not dead and hasn't dismissed me; incredulity at the coincidence; nervousness because I now have to tell my mother that I've found the daughter she claims to hate.

Yes.

"Hi," she said. "Do you mind me calling? Is it a good time?"

"Oh God," I say. "How are you? Where've you been?"

And she talks about how she and Roger moved to run a different motel, about how there have been divorces in the family, a couple of the kids have broken up with their spouses, and the grandchildren are having a rough time coping. And, most of all, how she knew her son didn't want to hear from her anymore, but she just had to talk, at least one last time. She'd tried a few times before, collect, long-distance, but no one had picked up the phone.

"Are you still angry at me?"

And I talk, apologizing for leaving the wrong impression

in her mind, of having been scared she'd been sick, or worse. Of life and work since we spoke last. Of watching Billy Ray. She had watched him earlier tonight too.

And, finally, talk of the other. The one Mo called "the incident." The one Mo asked her son not to find.

"I've got to tell you this," I say. "I found Rosalind. She's living in Texas. She's got two kids. Your grandchildren. She's married. She's happy. Her name is Cherisse now. Cherisse Fowler."

There is a whooshing sound on the telephone receiver, the sound of breath drawn in sharply. The sound of slow exhalation.

This is what my mother says: "Oh no."

A pause.

"She, she wouldn't just show up here, would she?" her mother asks.

Time now for reassurance.

"She's not going to do anything stupid. She's known about you for months. She's not going to blunder into your home. I know her. I like her. There's a bond between us. We're like brother and sister."

She says: "You are?"

Mo asks about Chuck and Heather, and what Cherisse is like, and "whether she's short and fat like me," and she laughs.

"Listen," I say, "she's thinking of writing you a letter." I don't tell her the letter is likely already in the mail and could arrive at her home tomorrow. She's already scared. Best not push her past breaking.

"That wouldn't be good," Mo says. "Roger picks up the mail. He'd wonder who it was from. Oh Rick, I'm scared. I don't know what to do. Help me. What should I do?"

My mother needs help from her first-born son. Help, to save her from her first-born daughter.

This is the help she hears from her son: "I don't know. I wish there was someone you could talk to, someone you could talk to face to face." Then, I suggest again that she reveal her past to her daughter Lori.

"You're the only one," my mother says, "the only one I can talk to."

Then: "Will you tell her that I called?"

Yes, I say. Yes, I will tell her.

She promises to phone again. And soon.

I pour a scotch and phone Cherisse.

"Oh my God," she says. "The letter is sitting on the kitchen table. I've been looking at it for days, wondering whether to send it, or just pick up the phone and call her. I've even dialled the number, but hung up before anyone answered. I addressed the envelope tonight, and put a stamp on it. I was going to mail it tomorrow."

Well, I say, she knows about you. The letter is a moot point now. I recount with as much detail as possible our conversation about divorces and grandchildren, about the family that is our family but not our family.

At that, Cherisse cries.

She recovers and says: "What should I do now?"

And, again, this is my answer: "I don't know. There's no point in mailing the letter — she already knows about you from me."

Too much has happened tonight. In the course of one television special and two telephone calls, a mother now knows that the daughter to whom she gave birth 38 years earlier is alive, is well, has a family of her own. She knows her daughter's name, and knows that her daughter knows of her.

She knows the children to whom she gave life are sharing each other's lives. Her secrets have met, and are secrets to each other no more. Scattered across the continent, three lives separated at birth converged tonight into one shared reality. There are those who say the truth shall set you free, but I picture our mother at home, afraid, thinking of her truths. Now we all know of each other. None of us knows what to do next.

G ood reporters constantly question themselves. How do I know what I think I know? What is fact, and what is assumption and supposition? Those are the questions I'd put to all my journalistic endeavors, spending hours pinning down arcane data and reinterviewing sources to determine that the story was there, that all the facts were lined up like ducks in a row.

The only story I hadn't put the question to was mine.

The facts, as I knew them, were that I was given up for adoption. That's the phrase everyone uses in the adoption business — *given up for adoption*. Some adoptive parents, afraid that their adopted kids might go looking for their biological roots, make up horror stories about mothers abandoning their babies in baskets left on church doorsteps, or in garbage cans. Honest adoptive parents like Ann and Fred Ouston tell truthfully that their adopted kids were "given up for adoption." It conjures visions of mothers tearfully signing legal documents, perhaps hugging their tiny sleeping babies one last time before leaving and getting on with their lives, content with the knowledge that they've done the right thing and have ensured their child will be raised by loving adoptive parents.

That was the vision I had about my life. I'd used the phrase "given up for adoption" in speaking and writing about my own story.

As it turns out, the phrase was not accurate.

I had not been given up for adoption.

I had been abandoned.

The truth was revealed in a rereading of the adoption order that turned young Paul Griffin into Richard Ouston. Now that the separate strands of my life history were weaving themselves into the warp and woof of whole cloth, I returned to the bulging file collected over the years to see if I had missed anything.

The adoption order was dated July 1957. I was two years old before being awarded to parents. Conversely, according to Cherisse's family history, baby Cherisse came home from hospital with her mother and father. Why was there so long a wait for me?

Ann Ouston, by now 75 years old, had forgotten the little details. "I'm sorry, Rick," she said. "I might have known, but I just forget."

It was sister Sharon, the keeper of our branch of the Ouston family's stories, who'd known the answer since first hearing her mom and dad talk around the kitchen table about how Sharon would be getting a new baby brother.

"Your mother never signed the legal documents giving you up," she said. "The courts had to declare you a ward of the state, an orphan, before they could grant the adoption. I thought you knew that."

Indeed, I should have known that. Part of the adoption order had included a line stating "the court doth order and adjudge that the consent to this adoption of the mother of the above-named infant, Paul Anthony Griffin ... be and is hereby dispensed with."

The phrase had meant nothing on first reading. At the time, I was looking for my parentage, not for discrepancies in adoption dates. The words hadn't registered on first reading. Now they made sense. And so did Mo's anguish.

With her first child, she'd completed the legalities of adoption. With her second, she'd cut and run.

My mother had vanished, leaving the baby she'd named Paul in hospital. She had not signed the paperwork required to "give a baby up for adoption." In the vernacular of crime writers, she'd left without a trace. That's why two years passed between my birth and adoption. It took those years of legal maneuvering to declare the infant Paul Griffin a ward of the state and to issue an adoption order granting parentship to Ann and Fred Ouston.

Mo must have known the law would place her baby into a home, and she likely had no idea that it would take two years for the law to waive her rights of parenthood and legally declare the infant adoptable.

The vague sense of abandonment I'd felt years earlier was now cast into sharper outline. In truth, I had not been given up for adoption. Mo had abandoned me. Just walked away. That's why she'd thought her child would hate her.

I was glad it had taken this long to figure it out. Had I known about the abandonment, my search may never have begun. The temptation to dismiss my missing mother as someone who had walked away from her flesh and blood may have been too strong. By now Mo had made it clear this had not been easy for her either. Her joy at being found was too obvious, it showed in her voice and on her face. When she thought her son had told her to stop calling, she'd understood it as the penalty she had to pay for dumping her baby.

Rereading the adoption order, I try to picture young Mo at the hospital, recuperating from childbirth, waiting for the father of her child to arrive in Vancouver, realizing finally that he never will. And she, finally, making up her mind to flee. Again. Running away. Leaving another love child in her wake.

She had said she loved me when I was born. That left me with two options: decide to hate her for abandoning a child, or try to alleviate her suffering by sharing it. The latter seemed the only acceptable choice.

But, having made that choice, it felt obvious that I would have to strike the phrase "given up for adoption" — and even the term "adoptee" — from my personal vocabulary. They are handy words to describe the facts behind the lives of those adopted, but by using them, society buys into the fiction that all relinquishing mothers had a choice to give a child up, instead of being forced by society to give up the right to be a mother. And not all of those adopted were carefully signed over to the state. Some of us, like me, were in fact left to be caught by whatever social safety net existed at the time.

Even the word "adoptee" places us into the realm of chattel — people who are defined by the adults who adopted us, even after reaching adulthood ourselves. No other adults are labelled by the actions of their parents, biological or adoptive. By accepting the terminology surrounding adoption, we lose sight of the realities faced by the biological parents at the time, and of any rights that adopted adults might have to learn about their pasts.

I had explored my past, and learned truths. Palatable or not, they were the truth, and my sense of personal history would have to be rewritten to accommodate those truths.

Mo was now an inextricable part of that history, and her regular calls resumed after the Billy Ray Cyrus night. Every couple of weeks or so, the Sprint operator with a collect call, Mo on the line saying she loves me, that she's scared.

"I love you, my darling," she says one early summer night. "But I'm scared. I feel like a schizophrenic, living one life with Roger here and another one with you. I feel like running away. I want to hide."

You ran away once before, I think to myself. But society said you had to. It wasn't your fault. I cannot say this out loud. I must not reveal that I know the truth.

I say: "When you gave us up for adoption you did the best you could do." Perpetuate the lie. The phrase is a balm, healing old wounds. It is time to stop the suffering. It is time to move on.

"Rick, I don't know what to do. I love you. When I had you, I loved you. I wanted to keep you, but I couldn't. When, when the Nova Scotia incident happened, oh Rick. I was in labor for two days. Two days! I asked the nuns for something for the pain. They said I should offer the pain up to God for my sin. For my sin! It hurt so bad. Then, finally, when she came along, I asked to see her. And they said no. I cried, and they said no, offer that up to the Virgin Mary."

It was the first time Mo had talked of her first born to anyone but herself. The memories, so long hidden, best forgotten, bubbled to the surface. The daughter she had borne was equated with pain, physical and emotional.

From friends and relatives, I know that the physical pain of childbirth can be ghastly, requiring drugs to alleviate some of the physical discomfort. Days after Mo's revelation, I came across an article, in a medical journal called *Pain*, about research performed at Montréal's McGill University. Psychologist Dr. Ronald Melzack found that the pain of childbirth ranks well above that of chronic back pain and cancer pain. In fact, on a pain index of 0 to 50, Melzack said, childbirth can rank at almost 40 — equivalent to a toe amputation without anaesthetic. Melzack said many women who are unprepared for the severe pain during birthing require psychological treatment afterwards because they suffer intense feelings of guilt and failure that leave them depressed and even suicidal. Even with drugs, forceps or caesarean sections, he said, many "women experience terrible, terrible pain and they are very angry." Younger women experience more pain than older women, and the lower a woman is on the socioeconomic scale, the greater the pain experienced. Mo fit the profile for what Dr. Melzack called "some of the worst pain ever recorded."

And the nuns had told her to pray.

I try to imagine Mo's emotions: remorse, fear, shame, loneliness, guilt, combined with physical pain. For more than 30 years they lay heavy in her gut. Mo would not be whole until she swallowed the past, digested it and came to terms with the present.

And still she referred to her daughter, to my sister, as "the incident."

Finally, after half a dozen calls, I snapped.

"Mom. Mo. She has a name. Her name is Cherisse. She's not an incident. She's a person. She's my sister. She's your daughter. We are brother and sister and are going to be brother and sister the rest of our lives. Don't call her an incident. She knows who you are and where you are and she's respecting your privacy. She deserves some respect too. She has a name. It's Cherisse. I wish you'd use it."

Mo paused.

I've insulted her. By blurting out my feelings I risk losing her. She feels great pain; Cherisse feels great pain. There is no easy way to achieve balance and relieve both of those pains. I am playing amateur psychologist. It is a dangerous game. A professional counselor might conclude that what I am doing is the worst thing that could be done, forcing a woman 59 years old to crawl back into her memory and face a demon long left behind. Perhaps this is cruelty of the highest order. But to do otherwise would be cruel to Cherisse, allowing our mother to play favorites. I don't know what is right.

She says: "Cherisse. It's a pretty name. I called her Rosalind."

It is the first time she has said the name of her daughter to another human being.

"Cherisse. It's a nice name."

And she asks about the children, Heather and Chuck, about Cherisse's life and times. Again I recount her losses, the murder of her father, the death of her mother, then her husband. She says: "She's gone through so much. Oh, my baby. Does she hate me?"

No, I say. She'd like to get to know you. She'd like to talk to you, and maybe see you one day. She understands what you went through. Then, without being asked, I tell my mother the phone number of her daughter.

"She hopes you'll phone her. She knows you'd phone collect." I knew that last Christmas Cherisse had gathered Robert and the kids around the kitchen table and told them that if there was ever a collect call from someone named Mo, they should accept it.

"I'll do it," says Mo. "I'll do it."

We hang up, her promising to call me once she fulfills her pledge.

In Texas, Cherisse and Robert are in bed, sleeping. It is past midnight. The phone rings. Robert picks up the receiver, hears the operator ask "Will you accept a collect call from Mo?"

He says: "Mo who?"

He hears a whispered voice, deep, gravelly, say: "Mo. It's Mo."

He says: "I don't know anybody named Mo."

He hears the voice say: "You big Texan, it's Cherisse's mom."

Awake now, Robert turns to his wife.

"Cherisse, wake up. It's your momma on the phone. It's Mo."

Cherisse takes the phone

"Hello?" she says.

"Hello my darling. This is the same for me as it is for you, so start crying and then stop so we can talk."

She has rehearsed the line.

Cherisse says: "Oh my God."

"No, my dear, it's not God. It's just your momma." She laughs.

Cherisse cries. Through ears foggy with sleep she hears her mother apologize for leaving her, hears about two days of labor pains, of a life spent wondering about the daughter she left behind, about being scared, about how she understood if Cherisse hated her mother.

From time to time Cherisse whispers "Oh my God." It is the only thing she can think of saying.

Then, she hears her mother say: "I love you." And she cries some more. Mo promises to phone again, during the day this time, as soon as she can, and she rings off.

Seconds later, Mo calls Vancouver.

"I did it," she says. Her son can hear his mother smiling half a continent away. "I did it. I told her I love her. I do. And I love you, my darling. You made this happen."

She tells me about Robert's sleepy response: "Mo who?" Already it's become a family story which will be told and retold, if only around a circle of three former strangers. About Cherisse's "omigods," and about the pledge to phone again. As soon as Mo rings off, another call. This time it's Cherisse on the line. She recounts her version of the conversation. I don't interrupt to say I know the story already. It was her call. The story belongs to Cherisse. So far, it is all she has of her mother.

That, and her life.

*I*t was during the coffee break on the second evening of a night school course I was teaching that my juvenile delinquent past came back to haunt me. An adult-education course, Introduction to Print and Broadcast Journalism, had attracted the usual mixture of bored office workers thinking of job changes, Generation Xers fantasizing about an EXCITING CAREER IN JOURNALISM! and earnest newsletter writers looking to hone their skills.

At the back of the classroom sat a tall, strikingly attractive retail worker named Christina Windsor. She hadn't said a word during classroom discussions, but sidled up to me on our way to the college cafeteria.

"We know each other," she said.

I drew a blank, trying to remember where and how. Recalling names and faces is not my specialty, but Christina could easily pass as a fashion model, and in my life I don't meet many fashion models.

"You crashed a house party I was in charge of in 1973 and came after my brother with a broken vodka bottle," she said.

My cheeks turned red. As a teacher, I'd tried to sell myself as a world-wise font of journalistic knowledge, someone to be respected. Now the twenty-year-old memory of being ordered out of a house by a tall, gorgeous twentysomething woman flooded back. It was true. As a teen, there had been evenings I had played wild boy. One night Christina's younger sister had thrown a party, word of it had spread around the high school we all attended, and some uninvited friends and I crashed it. There had been a long-running testosterone-fueled feud with her brother, the cause of which is long-since forgotten, and an attack aborted by the towering Christina. Sheepishly, I'd left the house party — having been ordered out by a girl — and left the memory behind.

Christina had never forgotten. She'd followed what career I'd had — the only time most classmates from our high school were in the news was when they were being convicted of a crime — and when she read that I was teaching the journalism course, she'd signed on. She'd also read some of the stories about my adoption reunion, and there were more unknown connections between us.

Christina's mother, the former Margarete Lapinski, had died the previous year. Just now, Christina was going through boxes of her mother's papers and pictures, and had come across photographs from the first job Margarete had after fleeing Poland during the war and arriving in Vancouver. Young Margarete worked in an orphanage in Vancouver, Our Lady of Mercy, in the late forties and early fifties. It was the orphanage for Catholic infants. Or, as Margarete noted on the back of some of her photos, the place for "homeless babies."

It was where I'd begun my life.

The records of the orphanage had been taken over by the provincial government twenty years earlier, but the Catholic archivist for the local archdiocese had told me that all Catholic babies born in the city and put up for adoption spent their first few weeks at Our Lady of Mercy. Christina had vague memories of being taken by her mother to the orphanage and playing with the babies. She would have visited in 1955 and 1956, during my stay. It seemed that every twenty years or so our lives would collide.

The photos from Margarete's collection were taken between 1949 and 1953, so there would be no pictures of the baby I was. But the tiny black-and-white shots afforded my first — and only — glimpse of the rows of white cribs and white-outfitted nuns which encircled my universe as an infant. Babies and toddlers stare at the camera, looking tiny and out of place. What is missing, of course, are the parents that show up in most family baby pictures. In their place are workers and nuns. On the backs of several photos, Margarete had written the names of the children, names which would have been changed upon their adoptions. That's a picture of Margarete on the cover of this book, holding a baby called Edward. The orphanage, a stately mansion on a large, treed lot in the toney Vancouver neighborhood of Shaughnessy, has since been demolished and replaced by smaller mansions.

The editor of the *Vancouver Sun*'s Saturday supplement, Max Wyman, agreed to run the photos as a picture essay in his section, with a headline asking: "Could this be you?" The idea was that some of the former babies, now grown, might recognize their faces or original names, and hence obtain their first look at themselves as infants.

As it turned out, one of the pictures was of Vancouver resident Dolores Hunt, a baby with some Asian features. Young Dolores had been taken home by a white couple, but they returned her to the orphanage. "She's too Chinese," the couple had said. An Asian couple also took baby Dolores home, but gave her back as well. "Too white," they'd said. With a mixture of Austrian, Hawaiian and Chinese heritage, baby Dolores was deemed unadoptable and eventually placed into foster care. Her original name of Dolores had never been changed, and for the first time the now-adult Dolores knew what she looked like as a baby.

The photo spread ran in the *Sun* on July 17, 1993, alongside a story written by me in the form of an open letter to B.C.'s minister of social services, who was in charge of adoptions. It contained a plea for the laws to be changed and files unsealed so other adoptees could know their pasts. The story was illustrated with a photo of Cherisse and me, taken during my first trip to Texas. The headline for the page was "Adoption: It's time to change the rules." Above the headline, editor Wyman had written: "On Sunday, Rick Ouston and his sister, Cherisse, will drive to their mother's home in Montana — and the three will be together for the first time in their lives."

Cherisse had flown to Vancouver the previous day. After Mo's initial phone call to her daughter, Cherisse and I had arranged to meet in my home town. From here, we'd drive through the Rocky Mountains and visit our mother.

There was one thing that Wyman hadn't mentioned: our mother didn't know we were coming.

Ten

_E_ven after two trips to Texas, Cherisse and I had barely had three hours to ourselves alone together to get to know each other. We felt a bond, true, imposed by genetics, inspired by choice, but there was so much we didn't know about each other. There had been no time to talk about those things which are deeply important to us, or even, and perhaps as necessary, the trivia that we hold dear, like hobbies and favorite songs and movies and dreams and fears and hopes.

So Cherisse decided to visit Vancouver, on her own, without Robert and the kids. They had talked about all driving up together for a holiday, stopping off at various U.S. roadside attractions along the way. But Robert felt she needed time on her own with her new brother. Although cash was tight, there was enough for one return airplane ticket. We'd been talking about her visit to Vancouver since the spring, when I was still trying to keep Mo's whereabouts a secret from Cherisse. Since then, Mo had phoned Texas, and her "incident" had metamorphosed into her living, breathing daughter.

Cherisse was on her way to Vancouver, the airline ticket

paid for, when she heard from her mother. There was no longer any need for brother and sister to plot how to tell mother about daughter. Now it was time for one last step. Cherisse wanted to meet Mo, to know what it is like to touch one's mother. To see her face and look into her eyes.

Mo had moved to Whitefish, Montana, a short flight away. I offered to pay for the airfare, but Cherisse declined. Not because she didn't appreciate the offer. Her reason was simpler: she is terrified of tiny planes. She thinks they will crash. The phobia extends to rides at amusement parks, even to traversing bridges. It is something we don't share. But one thing that we do share is a love of road trips, of getting into the car and driving along roads we've never seen, heading towards an adventure. This would be an adventure for both of us. Two orphans, heading down the road, to see their mother.

Meanwhile, the calls from Mo kept coming to my phone in Vancouver. Mo was nervous, afraid that she would blurt something out about her new-found daughter in front of her husband. The motel handyman's name was Greg, but for some reason she kept on calling him Rick. Roger was puzzled; Mo told him it was one of those things, a slip of the tongue.

"But every time something comes on TV about adoption, I just sit there and cry, tears rolling down my face, and Roger doesn't say a word, and I just turn to another channel," Mo told me.

Cherisse and I had three options:

❏ Ask Mo permission to visit and run the risk of her saying no;

❏ Simply announce that we were coming and risk

her working herself into a state of panic as she
awaited our dreaded arrival;
☐ Show up out of the blue, unannounced, and take
our chances.

The first option could close the door on any future
visits, the second could put Mo in a psych ward or wreck
her marriage, and the third meant risking getting to Montana and learning she was out of town and wouldn't be
back for a month. Option three could mean a wasted trip,
but it also ran the least risk for all concerned. Or, alter-
natively, we could phone one or two days before arriving
in Montana, telling her we're coming but reducing the sus-
pense as much as possible. We would decide when Cherisse arrived in Vancouver.

With the help of *Vancouver Sun* editor Wyman, I timed
my adoption story and photo essay to appear during Cherisse's visit. Saturday morning, I plunked the *Sun* in front
of her, saying, "You might be interested in the paper
today."

Cherisse flipped through the pages, a puzzled look on her
face, scanning stories, finding nothing that might interest
her. Until she hit on my story, and the photo of brother
and sister.

"It's us!" she yelled, grinning widely. "I've got that picture in a frame on my desk at work!"

Now we'd come full circle. Cherisse's husband had
arranged for a newspaper story about his wife's new
brother in his local Texan paper; today her brother was
able to return the treat.

And just as Cherisse had arranged for her new family
to meet her brother, today I would do the same for her.
I threw an afternoon party, inviting Ann Ouston and sis-

ters Sharon and Lorraine, and a passel of relatives and friends: cousins, nephews, the circle of friends who celebrate our birthdays together, journalism and publishing friends, and Wendy Ratcliffe, who'd spurred my search in the first place. Christina Windsor, whose mother worked at my orphanage, brought dessert. There was even an invitation to ex-wife Wendy, now a mom, happily remarried and a TV newsroom executive. She declined, but it felt good to have extended the invitation. It was like my entire lifetime was standing in my living room, smiling at Cherisse's accent, comparing our looks out of the corners of their eyes, sharing my joy.

I'd been worried that Ann and Sharon might feel threatened, even discarded or excluded. In truth, my personal concept of "family" had come to extend past the borders which surrounded the Ouston kids and their mom. It now included Mo and Cherisse and Cherisse's kin. And the next day Cherisse and I would leave, driving even further away from the old neighborhood and the old frontiers of what was once my family. The movies tell us one's first allegiance must be to one's family, but my allegiances were now divided — extending to others with whom I had not grown up, but with whom my life was now bound. They were my family now, those previous strangers who shared my blood. Not a replacement, displacing people who called me brother and son, but an addition.

And my friends were my family, too, people with whom I'd shared fears and successes and drunken singalongs. We were thirty- and fortysomethings now, most of us concerned with home renovations and child rearing, but now and then the old spark rekindled and spiffy dinner parties with matching china and learned observations would thankfully degenerate into competitions over who could hang a spoon off the tip of their nose the longest.

The people in the room were the family of my choosing. While contemporaries spent years of psychoanalysis coming to terms with the woes of belonging to a family that didn't measure up to Donna Reed's, I had managed to short-circuit that route by finding family on my own, and revitalizing at least some of what was already there with Lorraine. There are times when one feels truly grateful. This was one of those times.

There was only one person missing. We'd see her soon.

By the end of the day, only the diehards remained. Lorraine, Cherisse, cousin Janet — the daughter of the godparents who were listed on my amended baptismal certificate — and her friend Pam. We drove to a karaoke bar to continue the celebration. Lorraine and I had spent too many nights and too many dollars in similar bars during my visits to her home, singing loudly and pretending to be musical superstars. Lorraine does a passable Patsy Cline, and my Conway Twitty usually sparks applause. In truth, I think we both wanted to perform for Cherisse, to show off. But it was Cherisse who stole the show by mounting the stage with Lorraine to sing duet on Patsy Cline's "She's Got You."

It wasn't so much the singing talent that made me try to record a mental picture of the two short women to keep in my brain forever. Actually, both went off-key from time to time. But this is what I saw, watching them sing together: two women, both orphaned at birth, and again during their lifetimes — Cherisse through deaths, Lorraine through skewed societal mores — deciding to harmonize not only in song but in life. The smiles on their faces were genuine, displaying a sincere affection for each other, and for their brother listening and watching. I didn't want the night to end. We could have sung all night. But there was a long drive ahead of us the next day.

Y ou learn a lot about a person when you're stuck beside them on a fourteen-hour car trip. Often you learn to hate certain little things about them, and about what they do. Here is Cherisse's habit: she reads signs and billboards. Out loud. Every single sign she passes.

"Dunkin Donuts!" she exclaimed.

"Shoppers Drug Mart!"

"Bayside Market!

"Okanagan Resorts!"

There are a lot of signs between the west coast of Canada and Montana. She read every one. Out loud. It helps her pass the time. It helped drive me nuts. Finally, navigating a particularly treacherous mountain pass, I clenched my teeth, held out my hand palm downward and appealed in sign language for silence.

She got the hint. Until the next town.

"Dew Drop Inn!"

"Safeway!"

"Radio Shack!"

I love my new sister. I wish she'd shut up. For my part, I'm chain-smoking so furiously the air-conditioner can barely keep up. The nervous tension inside the car is almost as palpable as the cigarette smoke. We're off to see our mother. Our mother doesn't know we're coming.

There is still time to phone Mo, but brother and sister have decided to take our chances. It could be two days in a car for nothing, but we've decided it's best for Mo's nerves to just scare her all at once, instead of terrifying her in increments. If she refuses to see us, or allows just a quick glimpse, then we'll return to Vancouver and that will be that. In our first conversation I had promised her that I'd never just show up on her doorstep. But that was three years ago. Now there's someone else involved in our lives, and we in hers. The promise I had made during our first conversation meant spending more than a year convincing Mo that it was okay to see me. I didn't want to spend another year doing the same on Cherisse's part. More importantly, Mo had proven herself capable of handling herself emotionally both when I found her and when I told her about finding Cherisse. She wasn't psychologically fragile, just scared, and I felt that all she needed was prodding, and that she'd be happy once it was done.

Now we are in Whitefish. Mo has told me the name of the motel she is managing with Roger. The telephone book for the town she lives in tells us her home address is just a few doors up the road from the motel. We've booked a room with twin beds under a phony name and will stay at the motel our mother runs.

Cherisse and I plan what we'll do once we get to the motel. If Roger's on the desk, Cherisse will do the talking. Roger might have seen a picture of me, the one that ran with the *TV Guide* article I'd sent Mo back in 1990. I've grown a beard since then and my hair is longer, but my stutter could give us away; Cherisse's broad Texas accent will let us pass as just another couple checking into a motel. Once we are in our room, I will phone Mo at home and arrange to meet that night, or the next day. Or not at all.

If it's Mo at the desk, I'll go in alone to register and try to let her know that she should sneak up to our room later on when she gets a chance.

If neither Mo nor Roger are working the desk, it will be a snap to register. Whichever way we get a room, however, we'll have to pay cash: a credit card would identify us.

We feel like spies. In reality, we are. Spying on our mother. I park the car in the motel lot, and we walk to the door labelled "office." Cherisse does not read this sign out loud. Thankfully, there is a window by the front door. The man behind the counter looks like the man in the only photograph we've ever seen of Mo and her family. Cherisse turns around, grabs me with both arms, trembling.

"Oh God, it's Roger!" Then she laughs, loud. We hang on to each other for support. We are two children, about to spring a trick on our step-father. Only, our step-father doesn't know he's our step-father. I laugh too.

"Okay, kid. Let's do it," I say. "You do the talking."

As an investigative reporter, I've used false names and cover stories dozens of times to ferret out information. For Cherisse, however, this is a first. She performs admirably, giving Roger the name that the reservation is under. He goes through the desk clerk check-in patter — "How many nights? You got a car here?" — and doesn't even look up.

"Check-out time is twelve o'clock," he says.

By now I'm feeling cocky, and thinking that Roger might unwittingly reveal something about Mo's movements and whereabouts. I put on my best Texas accent and ask: "And when does the office open up, suh?"

Says Roger: "I'll be here at seven thirty in the morning."

"Long day," says I.

"I'm here til nine o'clock tonight."

It's now seven p.m. That means Mo is on her own for the next two hours. Roger has just told me the time to call her is now, or after seven thirty tomorrow.

Then, just to make sure, I ask in the same accent: "We-all might have to stay for another night, but we won't know until tomorrow. Can we-all call y'all then?"

"Yes," he says.

"And who should we'all ask for?"

"I'm Roger."

"Thank ya, suh."

Cherisse and I lug our bags upstairs, giggling. This feels less and less like James Bond, and more and more like Jim Rockford. My phony accent wouldn't have fooled anyone who could even spell Texas, but Roger fell for it. Or perhaps he was just following the code of a good desk clerk: don't ask what you don't want to know. And we can pretty well conclude that he doesn't want to know that the nice young couple he just checked in is actually the illegitimate children of his wife.

We lock the door. I sit on the bed and dial Mo's number. She answers.

"Mo, it's Rick. I'm here in Montana."

"Where are you?"

"At the hotel."

"Which hotel?"

"Your hotel. Room 212."

"Oh my God." A pause, and then, presciently: "Are you alone?"

"No."

"Who's with you?"

"I'd rather not say."

"Who is it?"

"It's Cherisse."

"Oh my God," she says. "Oh my God. Oh my God. I'm scared. Rick. I don't know what to do."

"Okay, calm down. You know you can trust me. You know that. We're in town, and we're just passing through. If you can see us, that's great. If you can't, we understand. If you can't see us, we'll take off. We're not going to bumble into your life. You know that. You can trust me. You know that you can trust me."

The sound of her breath is heavy on the phone line. She is trying to calm her nerves.

"Rick, I'm scared."

"Look, if you want us to go, we'll go. You don't have to do anything you don't want to do. If you don't want to see us, just tell me, okay?"

Another pause, then: "Roger's taking the dog out."

It takes a second for the significance of her remark to sink in. Roger is in the office. But she can see what he's doing. They don't live a few doors away. They live right here! She's one floor below us!

"I can only come up for a second. Watch for me!" And the line goes click.

Cherisse is standing in the middle of the hotel room. She's only heard my side of the conversation.

"She's on her way up," I say, walking to the door, opening it and leaning against the frame. Cherisse is frozen in the centre of the room, standing between the two beds.

"C'mon over here. This is why we came here."

"Rick, I can't."

I have to walk over to her, gently push her shoulders and guide her to the door. We stand, waiting, watching down the hallway, Cherisse in front of me.

The fire door opens and we can see Mo. We can see her smiling, and she jumps, a little skip, first the right leg, then the left. She is skipping down the hall like a kid.

"Hello, my darling," she says, arms reaching for Cherisse. She hugs her daughter tight, head against shoulder, then cocks her head back so she can see the face of the daughter she left in Nova Scotia in 1954. "You're beautiful," Mo says, and she kisses Cherisse on the lips and hugs her again.

It is the first time in our lives that we have all been together. It might be the only time. We walk into the room.

Mo is carrying a white tissue paper, balled and moist. She has been crying. She smiles and throws the paper into my face, like a mother fond of joking with a son. She hugs me, turns to Cherisse and holds her again.

"I've only got a minute. Roger will be coming back," she says, looking into Cherisse's eyes. "You're beautiful."

I ask: "Can you get away tomorrow?"

"I don't know. I'll try. I can't promise. I don't know. I've got to get back." She kisses Cherisse again, walks to the door, opens it, looks down the hall both ways, then slips outside. Cherisse looks at me and holds her arms out. I hug her and can feel her knees buckle and give way. She loses control of her muscles, or gives it away, and I am holding her up. She sobs into my shoulder. "Well," I say, "that's your mom. Our mom."

She bites back a sob, then giggles.

"Did you see her coming down the hall?" she drawls. "She looked like a little elf, skipping around like that! She's so tiny. Oh Rick!"

"Indeed. Very short and very happy. Very happy to see you."

We are both exhausted, physically from the length of the drive, emotionally from wondering how the reunion might go or if it would proceed at all. It has been at least eight hours since we've eaten, but there's one thing on both of our minds.

"Let's get a drink," we say, and we walk into the Montana night, headed for the nearest bar, where we will recount to each other, time and time again, each individual moment of the few moments we have just spent with our mother.

Later, back at the room, with a take-out bottle of tequila and a bag of gas-station junk food, we conduct a picnic of sorts on our beds, munching and drinking, knowing that our mother is just one floor below, probably lying in her own bed beside her husband, keeping her terrible secret. It strikes me that, although there was elation in Mo's steps down the hall, the joy could be replaced by terror tonight.

"Cherisse," I say. "What would you feel, how would you feel if that was all there was? If she couldn't see us tomorrow and we had to leave and that's all there'd be?"

"I'd understand, Rick. I'd understand why. At least we'd have that, at least I've finally touched my momma and seen her."

And we sleep, two orphans, one floor above their mother.

*I*n the morning we unlock the motel door and leave it ajar, hoping Mo will walk in. She does not disappoint us.

"Good morning, my darlings," she says, smiling. "I didn't sleep well at all last night, kept on waking Roger up, tossing and turning. He asked me if I was all right, if I was sick or something. I couldn't tell him, 'Well, Rick and Cherisse are upstairs and I'm thinking about them.' Every time he'd fall asleep I'd wind up crying to myself, but I couldn't let him hear."

Mo says we can meet at a nearby restaurant this afternoon at one o'clock. It is the only time she can get away. It won't be for long. A hug and a kiss on the cheek for Cherisse, and one for me. She raises her mouth to my ear and whispers: "Thank you. Thank you. She's so beautiful. I love you." And she is gone. Cherisse and I kill time buying souvenirs for her kids — T-shirts emblazoned with the name of the town where their grandmother lives, the grandmother they've never known.

We arrive twenty minutes early at the restaurant, and Mo is early too. We meet in the parking lot. Arm in arm, Mo in the middle, we walk inside. If anyone asks, Mo could tell them we're relatives from out of town. It wouldn't be a lie.

"Roger thinks I'm shopping. I've only got an hour," says Mo, nestling into her seat. She sits beside Cherisse on one side of the table. I am on the other side, facing the two of them. It is a good vantage point to see the sidelong glances they aim at each other, comparing chins and noses and cheeks, caressing each other with their eyes. Under the table, Cherisse and Mo hold hands.

To other diners, we're just another table of people. No one has a clue that the scene they're witnessing is a re-union of mother, daughter and son separated since birth.

Cherisse has brought along photo albums, pictures of herself growing up, of her son Chuck and daughter Heather, her husband Robert. She opens the albums on the table, and Mo flips through the pictures. She is seeing her new grandchildren for the first time, but her motions seem automatic, uninterested. Cherisse talks about her children, but Mo doesn't seem to listen. She looks at the photographs, but there is none of the joy that one would expect from a grandmother seeing pictures of the next generation.

Mo is not thinking of being a grandmother. The un-expected visit of her firstborn children has forced her to think back to when she was a child herself. These are thoughts and memories which she hasn't revisited for a long time.

Mo starts telling us about her pregnancies, Donald, her fear of what her mother would think if she'd found out. She is talking, gazing out the window, at a spot halfway to the horizon. She is looking into the past. A sudden realization comes to me as I watch her: This is the first time this 59-year-old woman has told anyone — anyone — about her first two children since leaving them. Listening harder now to the rhythms of her words, she sounds like the frightened girl she was when she left her first baby. The voice of a child, scared. Sad.

"My mother just wouldn't have accepted it," she says. "My father, he loved me. I was the apple of his eye. But then he died, and my mother blamed me." At seventeen, Mo had run away to escape a mother she describes as physically and emotionally abusive. Her father had even given her some money to help her settle into a new life. But Mo's mother tracked her down, went to the town she had moved to and demanded Mo return home. While she was gone, Mo's father suffered a heart attack and died at 62. "She never forgave me for having been away when my father died. If we hadn't been away, she said, he wouldn't have died."

Soon after, she got pregnant with Cherisse — the baby she named Rosalind — and moved away again. This time, her mother never tracked her down.

Cherisse gasps a little, inwardly, listening to the story. Her adoptive mother, too, blamed her for the death of her husband. The robbery at Thebeault Jewelers occurred in the late afternoon, at a time when young Cherisse used to help out in the back of the store after school. Stanley Thebeault had escaped the store into the street when the robbers appeared, but fearing that daughter Cherisse might still be inside and in danger, he went back in, calling for Cherisse. That's when he was shot and killed. Cherisse hadn't gone to the store after school that day. She'd visited a friend instead. Adoptive mother Eilleen never forgave her for that.

Mo looks at her daughter, not aware of this experience they have shared.

"When I was in labor with you, I was in labor for 42

hours. I asked the nuns for something for the pain, and they told me to offer my pain up as penance for my sins. When you finally came, I wanted to see you. I wanted to see your face. But the nuns wouldn't let me. I cried and cried, but they wouldn't let me see my baby. They told me to offer my tears to the Virgin Mary. But you weren't a sin. You were just a baby. I didn't feel like I had sinned, but that's what they said, the nuns, they said to offer my tears up for my sins."

Mo looks out the window again. Her face is expressionless, resigned. She is again feeling the pain. Physical pain from the labor of giving birth to a baby she never saw, emotional pain of having that baby taken away.

I feel like an intruder, watching this reunion between mother and daughter, gawking at something which I have no right to gawk at, this most personal of moments. I am the youngest at the table, but am feeling like the only grown-up here. Our mother is transported back to the joyless days of her youth. Cherisse is sharing with her mother the memories of herself giving birth, of what it must have been like to lie powerless as those in control snatched the baby away. Emotions that can only be shared by mothers, colored for Cherisse by the fact that this is still her first live conversation with the woman who is her mother.

We sit at the same table, but we have three separate points of view: Mo is a teenager again, having opened a door to memories long left closeted; Cherisse is only today meeting her mother and feeling like a child; I am the odd man out, ever the observer. This trip was designed as a gift to my sister — contact with her past. By coming here, I think, we've dragged our mother down a road too painful to travel. Maybe I've made a big mistake. But, almost as if she's reading my mind, Mo turns to me, smiles, shakes her head.

"This is all your fault," she says, falling back into the

role of kibitzing with a son. "I knew it would happen. I hoped it would happen. Every time someone comes to the motel from Canada, I've wondered if it's going to be you and Cherisse. A few months ago there was a man in the lobby, Roger was checking him in, and I got a glimpse from the office. He had long hair like yours, and glasses and a beard. And I felt my heart going into my throat, thinking, 'He's here! He's here!' I felt scared, but happy. But it wasn't you. I'm glad you both came.

"Look," she says, switching her gaze to each of her children. "There's something I want to bounce off of you both. You know how Roger reacted when he found out about Rick. Well, I can't tell him that I'd had a baby before him. He wouldn't take that well at all. But I've been thinking: What if I told him you were twins? That you were born the same time? What do you think of that?"

Cherisse and I look at each other. Unspoken in Mo's scheme, of course, is the hope that Roger would think she just "did it" once, that there'd been no one else of any significance before him. Our mother wants us to lie for her. To pretend we are twins, when we are not. But to combat one lie — that we don't exist, that Mo never gave birth — with another — that we shared the same womb at the same time — is no solution. Such lies have led to us three strangers being scattered across the continent. Cherisse lets me speak.

"No. Someone would find out, eventually. We'd have to hide our birthdates and keep up the pretext the rest of our lives. It wouldn't work. There have been enough lies. Roger would find out, eventually, and you'd be in worse trouble. No." Cherisse says nothing, but nods her head. "We don't want to cause you grief, you know that. If we can't be honest, then I'd rather do nothing at all."

Unsaid, but understood by all three of us, is that this

will likely be as good as it ever gets between our mother and her secret children. One day, Roger will die. That might happen before Mo's passing, it might happen after. But even when the threat of losing her husband is removed, our mother might not wish to alienate her other children with the facts of our lives. We will remain secrets. This meeting is just that — a meeting, to rectify that which had been left undone at the birth of Cherisse, allowing mother and daughter to see each other. It will go no further. At least not for now.

The conversation turns to small talk, about homes and jobs, hobbies and relatives, the lives of Mo's other children. The hour is quickly gone. It is time for our mother to return to her life, and us to ours. Cherisse has brought a camera, something I'd been unwilling to bring to our first meeting for fear of scaring Mo off. But Mo isn't scared of the camera. We take turns, passing the camera to each other for a quick snapshot — Cherisse and Mo, Rick and Mo — and getting a passing waiter to take a photograph of the three of us together.

Anyone looking at the pictures would see three fairly short people, smiling for the lens. They could be a mother with her now-adult children. They could be strangers, cast together for one time only. Cherisse has a set of prints, and I have a copy. Mo does not have photographs of us. It would be too dangerous to the life she has made.

*L*ate one night, weeks after returning to our homes, Cherisse phones me.

"Remember back in the hotel room, the first time we saw Mo, when you asked me if it would be enough if I just saw her that once, and I said 'Yes'? I didn't tell you the truth. From the day we first found each other, I'd hoped that I could get to know her, that my kids could have a grandmother, that we could get to know each other and visit each other and not have to hide. Rick, I don't want to be the secret one, the one that she can't talk about. If she can't tell her family about us, I don't want to have to hide and sneak around to see her. If we can't be up front and open, then I don't want to do anything more. You're my brother, and I'm your sister, and I love you, but if Mo can't be our mother, I don't want to have to pretend and wait for a phone call now and then in the middle of the night. I just don't want that."

Cherisse was echoing my own feelings of a couple years earlier, the feelings that led me to ask Mo to cut back on her phone calls. That request had been misinterpreted by Mo to mean that her son never wanted to hear from her again, and she'd cut off contact. I'd never shared those feelings with Cherisse, afraid I'd color her perceptions of her mother.

But son and daughter, separated by lifetimes and nations, had reached the same conclusion. We had done what we could, we had seen each other and our mother. That which was left undone was now done. Now, having touched and seen each other, at least we have, in the words of psychologists who research such things, "effected closure." The circle, which had been open, was now complete. There seems to be nothing left to do. Cherisse and I will continue thinking of each other as brother and sister. We can communicate at will, without deception, with pride in each other and each other's accomplishments. We will celebrate the holidays and visit each other and send gifts at will. We are part of each other's families, and will be forever. We wish our mother could join us, but wishes can't change the past.

Eleven

It was a few days before Christmas 1993, and I was trying to think of the best gift I could give my new sister and her family. Last year at this time I was in Texas; this year we'd share gifts by mail. One of the things about finding more family is you're on the hook for Christmas and birthday presents for life. It's a small price to pay.

I had given Cherisse context to her life, and that was good. She had returned that favor. I had given her a mother, albeit one who couldn't be a mother, but it was the thought that counted. There was something else I could give her, something only I could give her: her father. At least a photograph of her father, our father, now long dead. Mo had no pictures of Donald, the man she had loved. But there was someone who would — his son, Michael. I had written him twice now, the last letter including a photograph of Cherisse and me. There had been no reply.

It was time for direct action. So I phoned him. He wasn't expecting the call, but he didn't seem nervous.

"I got your letters, but I haven't thought about them much," he said in a lilting Newfoundland accent. "I showed them to my grandmother, the woman who raised me after my dad died. When we got your first letter, she looked at it and said 'Well, it might be true.' But when we got your second letter, and you said there were two of you, she said 'It's just a package of nonsense.' So, you have to respect the old woman's wisdom. She may be old, but she's still got her mind. So, that's why I never wrote you back or anything. I find it hard to believe you, if truth be known. So there it is."

The man speaking is my half-brother. He is casually dismissing the fact of my life with an indifference that is difficult to stomach. I cannot say this.

"Look, Michael, I'm not asking you to believe me. All I'm asking for is a photograph of your father. I'm not asking for anything else. I don't want anything else. One day maybe we'll get a chance to meet, if you want, but this isn't some kind of a scam where I'm trying to cash in on an inheritance or anything. I'm legit; I'm in the CBC phone book, for God's sake. I have some standing in the community. All I want is a picture."

He paused, finally asking: "Well, how can I know that the woman you say is your mother is telling the truth?"

"Michael," I say, "indeed, we can only take her word for it. But there's no reason for her to lie, and there were only two people there at the time. Only they know who they were."

"Oh, I know about the birds and the bees," he says. "Well, I'll take a look for you, but I can't promise you anything. D'you want to phone me back next week?"

It was a start. I promised to phone. But when I did, he didn't sound hopeful.

"The only pictures of my dad are owned by my grand-mother," he said. "I was just three when he died, and I don't have any photographs. She does, but she says she wants to talk to you first. She wants to know the name of your mother, to prove that your dad was who you say he was." And he gave the number of his grandmother. My grandmother.

An old lady's voice answers the phone. Old, but feisty. "Tell me the name of the woman," she says. "I know who my son was seeing back then. What was her name?"

Moral quandary. I have promised my mother to keep her secret. And supplying a name to an 84-year-old woman will not prove to her that Donald was my father. At best, this woman who apparently supplied part of my genetic heritage might remember that Donald and Mo had dated. At worst, she could expose my mother's secret to her relatives still living in Corner Brook.

"I can't tell you her name," I say. "I've given her my word."

"Well, she must be quite the character, your mother," the woman says. "Giving a baby away, then coming back looking for more. She must have been the shame of her family. And she was no virgin, apparently, your mother," she says.

"No, son, I can't accept you. You've got no proof. My son's in his grave, and there's no one to speak for him but me. I don't accept you. Tell me this: why didn't your mother get married?"

I could have said: because your son wouldn't do the honorable thing back then and marry her. That, instead, she fled Corner Brook and came to Vancouver and waited for him to come for her but he didn't. But these are things that can't be said. It was her only son, the one who was my father. In the quarter of a century since his death she's likely elevated him to sainthood. Instead I say this: "I didn't want to bother you, ma'am, and I'm sorry for disturbing you. Goodbye."

And that was my first, and probably last, conversation with my grandmother. She can't be blamed for her attitude, I suppose. It was prevalent then. As the old people die off, the old societal mores will die with them. But for now, this old woman is very much alive. It was her and her peers who drove women like my mother, and my sister Sharon, underground, into a lifetime of secrets and secret shame. As modern adoption trends continue, young girls who feel they need to give their babies away have access to open adoptions, where they can watch their children grow and perhaps create some kind of relationship with them as years go by. But for the women who gave birth to secrets like me, in the sixties and the fifties and before, unfortunately far too many of them continue to feel they must remain in the shadows, hidden from the life they gave.

Twelve

*F*inding family means you're on the hook for Christmas presents for the rest of your life. Which isn't such a bad deal, considering the return.

Having struck out on the photo of Donald, I visited a nearby Indian reserve to buy an armload of jewelry and trinkets for the Fowler family down in Texas. A hand-carved plaque for Cherisse, earrings for Heather, and for Chuck a gaudy bolo tie that would be suitably understated in West Texas.

Finding family also means sharing their grief.

On May 3rd, 1994, in Andrews, Texas, Charles "Chuck" Alen Stanley Combs died from a self-inflicted gunshot wound to the head. He was buried three days later, Father Francis Frey officiating. Chuck was not quite sixteen years old. His funeral was held at Our Lady of Lourdes Catholic Church. After the priest finished the funeral service, Heather read a poem written by a friend in memory of her brother, then turned on a ghetto blaster and played a tape that Chuck's stepfather Robert had made: Elvis Presley, singing gospel songs. Cherisse had told me young Chuck shared my passion for Elvis, and was proud of the

Chuck shared my passion for Elvis, and was proud of the photographs I had given him from a pilgrimage I once made to Graceland to visit the tomb of the King. In his eulogy, delivered between loud sobs, Robert said: "Now our King is in heaven, with the King. Two Kings, singing together in heaven."

The preceding chapters of *Finding Family* were written before his death. I thought this story was finished. As these words are being written, Cherisse, Robert and Heather are busy unpacking their belongings into a new home. They didn't want to ever revisit the house in which Chuck shot himself. I have just returned home after making a hurried trip to Texas to attend the funeral, and to offer what diversion I could to Cherisse and the remnants of her family. Our family.

The trip meant suspending my life in Vancouver, spending money I didn't have on airplane tickets and motels and car rentals. A tiny sacrifice, something that is expected of family. Long hours into the hot Texas nights spent with my sister and her friends and a parade of Fowler clan, trying to think of something, anything, to say between the waves of horrible emotion that cause Cherisse's face to contort into a mask of pain dripping with tears.

They say there's nothing so soul-destroying as when a mother buries her child. As children of whatever parents we have, most of us grow up expecting the day will come when our parents die. It is the natural order of things. We bury the old, nurture the young. A mother expects her children to grow, perhaps to succeed, perhaps to make her proud. Grandchildren. A continuance of the family line.

There will be no continuance for Chuck. For his mother, despite the platitudes from well-wishers that "everything will be okay," everything will not be okay. The death of a child does not go away. The agony of the absence should soften, in time. Humans are resilient. Cherisse has survived much loss already. But she never thought she'd lose her son. And she'll likely never know why.

There was no note. It was less than a month after rock star Kurt Cobain had died in a high-profile suicide, but Chuck's musical tastes seemed to run more toward old rock and new country than Cobain's band Nirvana. The events prior to Chuck's death indicate that he thought he'd just screwed up again and wasn't anything but a screw-up, and life just wasn't worth screwing up any more.

Chuck was not a model child. There had been run-ins with the police. Small violations exacerbated by parole infractions, shucking curfew, hitting on girls who did not want to get hit on. Counselling had been tried. Even a boy's ranch. His parole officer, Bob Galvez, told me Chuck was "emotionally troubled." The root cause will never be known. Cherisse suspects her son was sexually abused as a youngster by someone once close to her family in Galveston. Maybe true, maybe not, but Chuck's court file grew fat. Cherisse and Robert asked the courts for psychiatric help, and instead Chuck was locked for months in a tiny jail cell in Fort Stockton, waiting for a counselling facility to find room, stuck between the cracks of a judicial system that waits until troubled young men become hardened violent adults before offering assistance. At least, that's the way Cherisse sees it.

The day before the funeral, at an open-casket viewing at McNett Funeral Home, Cherisse looked into the face of her dead son and whispered: "You weren't a bad boy, Chuck. You were a good boy." Chuck wanted to be a marine biologist when he grew up. He'd told his mother that he was proud of his uncle, and that he wanted to make his uncle proud of him. Now that would not be.

A week before he died, Chuck's best friend and another

buddy were killed in a motorcycle accident. They had been buried just days before Chuck ended his own life.

The night before Chuck died, there'd been a family fight in the Fowler household. Chuck was dating a nineteen-year-old. Cherisse and Robert thought she was too grown-up for their young son. Chuck had told the girl he was seventeen. He was already chewing tobacco and cultivating wispy facial hair. He wanted to be a man. His mother told him he wasn't. They were in each other's faces, yelling. Chuck rolled his fingers into a ball, made a fist and moved his arm back. Robert saw the physical threat, the two rolled around on the floor. No punches were thrown, but it looked like the violence might escalate. Cherisse called the police who came to the house and broke things up. Away from his parents, Chuck told the attending officers that he loved his mother, he loved his stepfather, and that he took full responsibility for having screwed up. Because of his record, police took him to the Andrews County Sheriff's Department, where he spent the night in jail. Because of the record, he was taken by police to the court house the next morning for a hearing to determine what would happen next in his young life.

Outside the courtroom, he ran. Down the street, around the corner, gone. Someone saw him taking off down Avenue B, heading toward his girlfriend's. She wasn't home.

As soon as he heard the news, Robert drove as quickly as he could to the Fowler house. Like most other Texans, he kept guns in the home. The constitution protects the right to bear arms, all 217 million of the guns that are estimated to be kept by United States citizens. Robert had taken precautions. The guns, the bullets, the ammunition clips were all stored separately. Chuck knew that too. Robert arrived at the house and opened the front door and saw his son sitting on the love-seat with the gun pointed at his head and heard the gun go off. Ambulance crews took Chuck to Permian General Hospital where doctors determined that there was no brain activity. The life-support system was shut down and Chuck took his final breath at 11:02 p.m.

We turn to friends and family when things go wrong, for advice on what to do next. For most human conditions there are words of counsel that can help a person figure out how to make things better. Not for death. Words can't bring back those who are gone. Words can help patch up some of the void, but only a bit, and only temporarily. The hole is still there. I tell my sister: "I'm supposed to be the one with all the words, and I don't have any words for this." She laughs, a small laugh, then she cries. We hold on to each other, tight hugs to allow Cherisse to at least feel the physical presence of her brother while she mourns the death of her son. We hold hands, hold each other, not knowing what to say, knowing there is nothing of significant value to say.

In Andrews, the local newspapers carried obituaries for Chuck. One paper said he died "after a short illness." Another noted simply that he died. No mention of the cause. The cover-up of North America's second largest killer of teenagers continues. Suicide is the second most frequent cause of death among white teenage males in Canada and the U.S., second only to accidents, ahead of homicides and far ahead of any trendy disease of the week, according to statistics from both countries. But we don't talk about the ancient taboo. Despite the silence, our children die.

Before this week there were three people in the world I could talk to who shared my blood. Now, there are just two. I feel anger toward my dead nephew. First I find family, then I lose family, all because a kid figured he knew it all and knew it all wasn't worth living for. Anger, for myself, for my loss. Anger because Cherisse hurts, her sobs and moans discordant in the pit of my soul. I don't want my sister to hurt, but there's nothing I can do about it. Anger. And sadness. Sadness for Cherisse, because she hurts. Sadness for Chuck, for what he might have been, and for the turmoil he must have felt in his kid brain.

It was from the chaplain with the Andrews police department that I heard about Chuck shooting himself. He had left a message on my answering machine, advising me to call the hospital. "It's an emergency," his message said. By the time I got through to the hospital, the life-support machinery was turned off and Cherisse was waiting for her son to die. She asked me to come to Texas, to be with her at the time of her need. In truth, I didn't want to go — there was nothing I could do, I thought. But she wanted me there, and it was where I belonged, consoling my sister, sharing her anger and her bitterness and her sorrow. It is what families do. We will probably share more grief during the rest of our lives together. There will be joyous times, too, to temper the pain. Whatever the times, we are together, joined by bonds of blood that cannot be unbound.

We will stay that way.

A couple of days after the funeral, I had to return home. It was Sunday, the second Sunday in May. Mother's Day. There would be no celebration for Cherisse. And although the subject of our mother had not come up between us during my stay — the first time we had not raised the fact of our secret mother during conversation — I couldn't help thinking on the drive to the airport about Mo. She had lost a grandson she'd never known and now will never know. And she doesn't even know about it. I wonder, if she calls again, should I tell her about Chuck's death? To hide it would be to perpetuate the lie. Finding family means, ultimately, losing family. And our mother will have to grieve for two generations who live, and die, in the shadows of her life.